Hospital for Sinners

Tom Wright

WIPF & STOCK · Eugene, Oregon

Wipf and Stock Publishers
199 W 8th Ave, Suite 3
Eugene, OR 97401

Hospital for Sinners
By Wright, Tom
Copyright©2007 by Wright, Tom
ISBN 13: 978-1-5326-5428-2
Publication date 3/27/2018
Previously published by Publish America, 2007

DEDICATION

This book is proudly dedicated to all the individuals who have been swindled by ungodly preachers and charismatic frauds to the furtherance of their own selfish end. May God hold these imposters greatly accountable in both word and deed.

For the love of money is the root of all evil: which while some coveted after, they have erred from the faith, and pierced themselves through with many sorrows.
1 Timothy 6:10

ACKNOWLEDGEMENTS

My sincerest thanks go to these friends who have greatly assisted me in completing this project that has been in the works for over thirty years: Dr. Al Cooke's, PhD, counsel and work on the photography was a tremendous help; Dr. Beverly Fletcher, EdD, began the editing process; Dr. Roger Firestein, PhD, was an invaluable aid in the early writing stages; and my son, Seth Wright, put hours upon hours of research and did the laborious task of obtaining permissions for this publication. Thank you all.

TABLE OF CONTENTS

ACKNOWLEDGEMENTS 5
PERMISSIONS 9
PREFACE 11
FOREWORD 13
INTRODUCTION 15

CHAPTER 1
GOD IN THE WHITE HOUSE 17

CHAPTER 2
CHRISTIAN COALITION 21

CHAPTER 3
MORAL MAJORITY 29

CHAPTER 4
ORBIS UNUM 35

CHAPTER 5
FIRST AMENDMENT 51

CHAPTER 6
ELECTRIC CHURCH 62

CHAPTER 7
SPECTATOR SPORT 95

CHAPTER 8
BIG BUSINESS 118

CHAPTER 9
PROPHETS, PRIESTS AND PRETENDERS 153

CHAPTER 10
TRUE SAMARITAN 169

CHAPTER 11
LIBERTY UNIVERSITY: GOD OR MAMMON 185

CHAPTER 12
LAST DAYS 201

ENDNOTES: 217

PERMISSIONS

Richard Bennett:
"The Adulation of Man in the Purpose Driven Life."

Jack Kinsella:
"America in Bible Prophecy."

Steven Mitchell:
Prometheus Books

Paul Proctor:
"The Falwell Faux Pas: Another Towering Inferno"

Cuttingedge Ministries:
"TBN: Temple of the Greek God and Goddess"

Dial-The-Truth Ministries:
Quotes and Testimonies

In Plain Site Ministries:
Quotes

All references and quotations from the Bible are taken from the *King James Version*.

The author believes in the "fair use doctrine" and that information is to be shared freely. Permission is granted to quote from this book—merely give credit.

PREFACE

Christianity began as a personal relationship with Jesus Christ. When it went to Athens, it became a philosophy. When it went to Rome, it became an organization. When it went to Europe, it became a culture. When it came to America, it became a business.

Hospital For Sinners is the culmination of nearly thirty years of planning and preparation. The idea was first conceived in the late 1970's; thus, we have a storied history of the *religious right* and its components from 1979 to 2006. During this time period the supposedly *light of the world* has become darkened by sex-scandals, misappropriation of funds, and sundry other lewd behaviors.

History should be a lesson to us all; however, these problems still exist and are inherently on the rise. Biblically and theologically ignorant church-goers still do not see the light; whereas, real honesty, integrity, and accountability is spiraling downward at an increased rate.

Our church leadership are in pursuit of money and power, while hiding behind a mask of self-righteousness and political associations. Does God want Christians to clothe themselves in sackcloth and ashes? No! Nor does He desire one to ride around in a Rolls-Royce either.

There is a generation, whose teeth are as swords, and their jaw teeth as knives to devour the poor from off the earth, and the needy from among men.
Proverbs 30:14

FOREWORD

*I hope I shall possess firmness and virtue enough
to maintain what I consider the most enviable of
all titles, the character of an honest man.*
—George Washington

It is perplexing for me to believe that men and women who broadcast their preaching to the world in the name of God would lie and deceive in their own self-interest. These charlatans of the worst degree will stand in front of TV lights with a microphone and deceive their followers in order to take their hard-earned money. They portray a form of godliness to increase their own personal wealth. These individuals display the following distinguishable characteristics:

1. They sell religion.
2. They continually pursue lavish lifestyles.
3. They preach politics.
4. They preach a continual message of health and wealth.
5. They abuse authority and use power control.

These so-called ministers of the gospel are no more than CEOs of large corporations who serve not to enhance God's heavenly kingdom, but merely to enrich their own earthly treasures and future legacies. They will achieve this goal by acquiring power through great wealth, harnessing a large following and embracing politics. The ultimate goal of this narrow-minded and biased brand of Christian fundamentalism is to move America towards its own brand of a humanized theocracy.

My desire is that this book will serve to enlighten the followers of such false prophets and give public disclosure to the immoral fundraising tactics and political involvements of "the conservative religious right" and its coalitions.

> *But, beloved, remember you the words which were spoke*
> *before of the apostles of our Lord Jesus Christ;*
> *how that they told you there should be mockers in the*
> *last time, who will walk after their own ungodly lusts.*
> —Jude 17, 18

INTRODUCTION

*For the time has come that judgment must begin at
the house of God.*
—I Peter 4:17

Never in recorded history have there been so many attempts to penetrate spiritual avenues as there are today. Westerners are on an intense search to find that extra dimension to fill the void in their lives. Church membership is at a high level and yet moral standards are rapidly declining. Why are many of our churches and its members engaged in worldly concepts and philosophies, seeking temporal earthly treasures rather than the eternal celestials? Is it possible that most so-called Christians say they believe but really do not? Nearly thirty years ago a sagacious and aged college professor told me, "Tom, if you want to make money in this life, then sell pornography or sell Bibles." This is sad, but true.

Recent polls indicate that there are more than sixty million 'born again' Christians in America. This country has ninety-five percent of the world's preachers and only five percent of its population. Our student enrollment in Christian schools, colleges, and seminaries doubles the rest of the world. The total radio and television time of gospel broadcasting exceeds the rest of the globe, while over forty million Americans attend church in an average week.

America is "united as one nation under God," and at the same time suffering from economic, social, and moral decay. I believe prosperous religious leaders are responsible because of the following scriptural words: "You are the salt of the earth; but if the salt has lost its savor, wherewith shall it be salted? It is thenceforth good for nothing, but to be cast out, and to be trodden under foot of men" (Matt. 5:13). We are now presently being stepped upon by our oil suppliers, broken alliances, and most of all, terrorist countries.

We have erected majestic cathedrals, encrusted them with rubies, humanized and fraternized the masses in order to assure a large following. Christianity has donned the cloak of self-righteousness, put prosperity on parade, and thus, destroyed the average local assembly by a terminal disease called 'materialism.' Priests and preachers alike are 'selling religion' in order to get anyone who can walk or crawl down an aisle to accept a Savior in whom they have very little faith themselves. But, is this the church?

When Martin Luther nailed the ninety-five theses on the castle church door in Wittenberg, he did not want to destroy the church or the system, but merely to correct some internal problems and reform the church council of errors. His primary desire was to rid her of carnality, political entanglement, a selfish search for salvation, and to restore to the church a love for God, for one's neighbor, and the Bible as the Word of God. This movement of magnitude, the Reformation, overflowed and America was born. Religious freedom blossomed and bore much fruit. Throughout the years, however, our religious heritage has become powerful, political, and prosperous, while at the same time more apostate!

Our great nation has root problems that stem not from Wall Street or Foreign Markets, but totally within the spiritual realm of worship. Religion has become carnal, our churches big business, and many of its leaders lustful and greedy. Many have turned their religious corridors of power into a Hospital for Sinners!

And Jesus said unto them, it is written, my
house shall be called the house of prayer,
but you have made it a den of thieves.
—Matthew 21:13

CHAPTER 1

GOD IN THE WHITE HOUSE

*Everyone thinks of changing humanity and nobody
thinks of changing himself.*
—Leo Tolstoy

Our Founding Fathers have been moaning from the grave ever since the Republicans announced a new "religious war." These so-called conservative Republicans and religious fanatics believe "traditional values" have been placed on the back-burner and replaced with money, corruption, and liberalism. They do not see their own failings nor understand real religious freedom.

Freedom of religion in America means more than mere freedom to worship and to believe; it gives us the power to disseminate our belief to others. Thank God for the religious freedom in America, where there is a greater diversity of religions practiced than any other country in the world. Where probably seventy-five percent of these religions are spiritually damaging or morally wrong, or both, they are still far better than a state religion.

For example, consider the country of Iran. A land whose national religion and a spiritual leader—often called Ayatollah Khomeini, which translated means "voice of God"—is usually a murderer and dictator. Even with our wide array of cults, isms, and spasms, we do not need this kind of situation in America, nor do we need religious pressure groups or coalitions of religious conservatives attempting to control our mode of thinking. God is not Caesar.

"Fundamentalism"

"If religion is the opium of the people, fundamentalism must be the amphetamine. Nothing excites the central nervous system of the susceptible body politic more effectively than a dose of that old-time, God-fearing, fire-breathing religion. The awesome energy generated by conversion, confession, commitment and rebirth is hardly used up by church work and charity. Much of it throughout U.S. history has been directed to political ends."[1]

Churches should emphasize "right living," love thy neighbor, spirituality, and avoid the corrupt enticement of political power. Prior to the 1970s, fundamentalist preachers denounced sin and evil in "the world" in order to compel their flocks into strict isolation from it. Nowadays those same jeremiads are beckoning people to a stern call for social action. "When I was growing up," recalls fundamentalist Pastor Rosco Gephard, "I always heard that churches should stay out of politics; now it seems almost a sin not to get involved."

When former President Jimmy Carter won the election in 1976, many church leaders—namely fundamentalists—felt that this Southern Baptist Sunday school teacher from Georgia was not a worthy Christian. History has shown, however, that Jimmy Carter is probably the finest humanitarian to hold that office in the past several decades. In contrast, the "Moral Majority," the "Christian Voice," or the "New Right"— coalitions that sprang up after the 1976 election—have not produced any great heroes either.

The conservative religious right helped elect Ronald Reagan and George Bush—father and son—to the White House. The former went to war with Iraq over Kuwait and was handsomely rewarded by their government after being defeated for re-election in 1992 by Bill Clinton. Today we have George Bush, Dick Cheney, Halliburton, and a new war in Iraq along with Afghanistan. Now, do not consider me unpatriotic for I fought in another war—Vietnam—that was publicly controversial and received a bronze star for my services. Our oldest son has served two tours of duty in Iraq; thus, the Wright family believes in fighting for freedom, but not for money and oil.

Church teaching should be concerned with the supernatural order and the sacred, not the natural order and the secular. "The natural order comes into the purview of religion only insofar as what is done in the natural order affects one's standing in the supernatural order. Just as the military says, 'leave war to the generals;' so too businessmen would say, 'leave business to businessmen;' and politicians, 'leave politics to politicians.' Indeed, if there is a real distinction between the natural and supernatural orders, the only legitimate concerns of religion as such in the natural order are the individual morality of those who act in the natural order and the freedom of the church to carry out its functions."[2]

"The GOP"

For the past thirty years the "religious right" has sought to put religion into the Republican Party. If we believe in the separation of church and state, then religion should not be tied to a Republican or Democratic platform. Our Founding Fathers built the "wall of separation" between church and state, and still today it remains as one of our best defenses freedom has ever had. Not all of our Founding Fathers were pious and "God-fearing men;" thus, they designed a republic in which all men—particularly themselves—would have a country to grow and prosper. Today's Republicans, for this and other reasons, should be far more grateful than they appear to be. Their patriarch, namely Abe Lincoln, refused to join a church, stating, "When you show me a church based on the Golden Rule as its only creed, then I will unite with it." Another Republican, Ulysses S. Grant, exhorted his countrymen to "keep the church and state forever separate" and strongly opposed the use of any public money to be allocated for parochial education—an issue the Republican platform endorsed in the 1992 election. Even George Washington would rumble in his sleep hearing the constant emphasis on "Judeo-Christian values" and of a "religious war" in the name of God, country, and traditional values. He once wrote, "Every person in this land has abundant reason to rejoice and to worship God according to the dictates of his own heart."

"Christian Politicians"

It has been said that if politicians are not dishonest when they go to Washington, they will be six months after arriving there. This is why new voices from mainstream Protestant churches feel represented by neither religious right fundamentalism nor the old religious liberalism.

If religious faith and Christian politicians make for better government, then our political pursuits should be more moral, honest, and sensitive to those without voice or power. However, this is where the "religious right" has failed. Since the late 1970s powerful religious coalitions have polarized political debate and made it less sensitive to the poor and downtrodden.

Does the "religious right" know its history? Evangelical Christians from a century ago were leaders in the "human rights" movement. They were tireless in their efforts working for the poor and the oppressed, and serving as advocates in the struggle for "women's rights." Is the "religious right" today benefiting the disadvantaged or are they chasing selfish goals and ambitions?

"True evangelical faith focuses on the moral values that must be recovered to heal the torn political fabric; ideological faith would rend the fabric further in the pursuit of power. Evangelical faith tries to find common ground between warring factions by taking the public discourse to higher ground; ideological faith fuels the rhetoric of 'us and them' and breeds a climate for hate and even violence. Evangelical faith holds up the virtues of compassion and community; ideological faith appeals to personal and group self-interest. Evangelical faith understands our identity as the children of God as a call to humility and reconciliation rather than the basis for attacking those who are less righteous."[3] We all care deeply about family and moral values within our society, and the erosion of character and responsibility in our neighborhoods and nation. Biblical virtue, not politics or Christian coalitions, is the only answer.

The church has the power to transform our nation into what most of us would like it to be. But it will not do so if it joins another religious crowd, which said 2,000 years ago: 'We have no king but Caesar.'

—Cal Thomas

CHAPTER 2

CHRISTIAN COALITION

"The mission of the Christian Coalition is simple. It is to mobilize Christians—one precinct at a time, one community at a time—until once again we are the head and not the tail, and at the top rather than the bottom of our political system."
—Pat Robertson

Pat Robertson and Jerry Falwell—Republican political entities—have been and are presently the two main personalities behind the "conservative religious right" movement in America. They have contributed greatly to religion; however, they have done very, very little for Christianity. This is primarily due to the fact that politics and powerful acquaintances made in Washington, DC have entered the pulpit. They have sought power, fame and wealth instead of seeking a Christ-like life.

Robertson, unlike Falwell, resists the label "television evangelist." Instead, he seeks to present himself as a Christian businessman, lawyer, and an expert in economics. He is, in fact, a Yale Law School graduate and the son of the late Willis Robertson, democratic senator from Virginia, who somehow learned to talk out of both sides of his mouth and smile all at the same time.

Pat Robertson is a very wealthy man. Some estimates put his net worth at over 140 million dollars. Pat Robertson, the evangelist, is a "jet-setter" and lives the lifestyle of a king. He crisscrosses the country in a BAC jet entertaining black-tie dinners, wearing expensive three-piece suits, and charging five hundred dollars per plate for a ten-dollar meal. Robertson rides in fancy limousines, sleeps in plush hotels, eats exquisite cuisine, and takes exotic vacations at remote resort areas around the world. He lives on the top of a Virginia mountain in a huge mansion with a private airstrip. He owns the Ice Capades, a hotel, diamond mines, and until recently, International Family Entertainment, parent company of the Family Channel. How does a televangelist, who is supposedly involved in nonprofit work, manage to create such a fortune for himself? Apparently, between dealing with murderous dictators and ripping off senior citizens, it is not that hard. Robertson seems to possess more of an interest in the wallet than in the eternal soul; the "here and now" is seemingly very important to him.

"Unseemly Business Ventures"

Pat Robertson's zeal for profitable business ventures led him to start the American Benefits Plus/Kalo Vita (ABP). This was a multi-level marketing scheme along the lines of Amway and Avon. Beginning in 1991, Robertson recruited people across the country to sell coupon books, some of who were retirees. He had more than twenty thousand "employees" for ABP. He set up seminars to train attendees and used the claim that the program was backed by Biblical principles. He insisted that they could earn between fifteen and twenty thousand dollars monthly. American Benefits Plus/Kalo Vita were unsuccessful. His attention shifted to changing the focus of the business. The company name was changed to Kalo Vita, a vitamin selling venture.

People were left with many coupon books unsold and tried to send them back to the company and get their money refunded. The company refused to refund their money. One seventy-six year-old woman, stuck with seven thousand dollars worth of coupon books, had to refinance her home. The company was another of Robertson's scams aimed at increasing his wealth by any means. An investigation later disclosed that CBN had "loaned" money to APB during its founding—almost three million dollars. Pat Robertson continues to use non-profit, donated funds for his ventures without regard to how badly it looks. It is shameful that he has a loyal following who send in thousands of dollars in support to CBN to, they believe, "promote the gospel." Those people need to be made aware that it is highly likely their money is being used to increase the wealth of Pat Robertson, not promote the gospel as they may believe.[4]

"Media Mogul"

Pat Robertson founded the Virginia Beach based Christian Broadcasting Network (CBN), a cable network that reaches nearly forty million homes, and is the primary source of income in donations to the organization. The annual budget of the Robertson organization is in excess of 400 million dollars. Much of this money is the fuel behind the Christian Coalition—the religious right—that funds and supports politicians and issues that fit into their particular mold. According to Christian Century, Robertson and the Christian Coalition were able to "raise over thirteen million dollars in order to become a major player in the 1992 primary and general elections. Working with other conservative evangelical groups, such as Phyllis Schlafly's Eagle Forum, Randell Terry's Operation Rescue, the Traditional Values Coalition, the American Families Association, and the Christian Voters League—Christian Coalition supporters staffed phone banks, walked precincts and distributed voter guides in campaigns across the country."[5]

"Christian Broadcasting Network's viewership has tripled since 1981, when Robertson switched from an all-religion schedule to a family entertainment approach, combining Christian shows with wholesome reruns (i.e., Flipper, Father Knows Best), westerns, old movies, and game shows. Recently, the network premiered CBN News Tonight, a regular evening newscast produced in Washington, with special emphasis on right-wing issues."[6]

Ice Capades, a traveling ice skating show owned by Olympic Gold Medalist Dorothy Hamill, was acquired by Robertson's entertainment empire. International Family Entertainment, Inc. (IFE), a spin-off of Robertson's Christian Broadcasting Network, made the purchase. The IFE's chief executive is Tim Robertson, Pat Robertson's son. The for-profit venture emerged from CBN in 1990 and began selling stock to the public in 1992. It operates the Family Channel in the United States and the United Kingdom. International Family Entertainment (IFE), a cable channel that carries a mix of original and rerun shows, is still home to Robertson's "The 700 Club"—a so-called nonprofit organization. Is it really not-for-profit?

In February 1995, IFE announced that it would produce four PG-rated feature films for theater release per year under the name of Family Channel Pictures. Anthony Thomopoulos, president of the television production arm of Steven Spielberg's Amblin Entertainment, was hired by IFE to head the film venture as chief executive of its entertainment subsidiary. The first series were released in 1996. Tim Robertson called the move "something of a shift in the focus of the company. We are admitting that to take our company to the next level, we've got to work more within the Hollywood system."

In the year 1995, the Federal Election Commission (FEC) filed a complaint against the Virginia Beach-based organization. In the complaint the FEC accused the Christian Coalition of raising money as a tax-exempt entity but spending it on pro-Republican activities without registering as a political group. The Democratic Party filed a similar complaint three years earlier—October 1992—against both Christian Action Network and the Christian Coalition. Even more serious than this, however, is the misappropriation of donated monetary funds by God's people that was not used for evangelization and the furtherance of the gospel.

"Dictator Allies"

In 1985 many critics charged that Robertson's prayers and political ties did not amalgamate. His mild-mannered style and affirmation to Reagan Administration policies also included Central America. The critics say that the relief arm of Robertson's CBN, Operation Blessing, supported the contra guerrillas who fought the Nicaraguan Sandinista government. This was the beginning of the Pat Robertson and Ollie North fraternity.

That and other allegations are summarized in the October issue of *Sojourners Magazine. Sojourners* states that, "millions of well-meaning U.S. Christians are donating money that is serving, directly or indirectly, to sustain Nicaraguan Contras and to perpetuate ... contra terrorism."[7]

Operation Blessing has given several million dollars worth of food, medicine, and other aid to Central America. One CBN news release announced a 20 million dollar effort to send aid to Honduras, Guatemala, and El Salvador.

While no one has publicly accused the organization of supplying contras with direct military aid, some critics argue that in certain circumstances, the line between humanitarian assistance and military aid is easily blurred. They say guerrillas can spend more of their own resources on guns if their families are being supplied with food and medicine.

Perhaps *Sojourners*' most serious charge involved a three million dollar donation that Operation Blessing allegedly made to the Nicaragua Patriotic Association. That organization's leader is known to have ties to the contras."[8]

Numerous other politically conservative Americans, however, believe that Robertson is so candid concerning his political views, that it may be that many financial supporters to Operation Blessing are not misled.

Nevertheless, aid of any kind to the contras would violate Neutrality Acts, which prohibit any support for the overthrow of governments at peace with the United States.

I was beside myself to learn about Pat Robertson's friendly relationship with now-deceased dictator of Zaire, Mobutu Sese Seko, former dictator of Guatemala, Jorge Serrano, and ruler of Zambia, Frederick Chiluba. I wondered what could possibly have attracted him to these dictators, all of who have notorious reputations as iron-fisted rulers who have pillaged and murdered their country's people.

Mobutu ruled by controlling his people with fear, intimidation, and violence. He became one of the richest men in the world. He could have written one check and fixed many of Zaire's ills. During his dictatorship, the country had little to no individual freedom. As in most dictatorial societies, demonstrations were illegal, journalists were murdered by the state, and most religious groups were banned. In fact, the U.S. State Department banned Mobutu from the country.

Pat Robertson's relationship with Mobutu was based on one thing: he had an opportunity to make a lot of money in Zaire. Zaire is a country rich in resources. Robertson knew that a partnership with Mobutu to start a diamond mining operation could earn him millions of dollars. He started the African Development Company (ADC) and began shipping diamond mining equipment to Zaire using the non-profit CBN's Operation Blessing aircraft.

He also tried to get the State Department to lift the ban on Mobutu's visa. Robertson became very amiable with the Zairean leader even to the extent of flying to Zaire on Mobutu's jet. He cruised on the Mobutu yacht, and dined at the presidential mansion. Against the wishes of many of his supporters and advisers, Pat Robertson continued to pursue the friendship with the known terrorist leader. The ADC turned out to be an unsuccessful venture. Mobutu died in September of 1997 after being deposed by a rebellion.

Pat Robertson's Guatemalan associate, Jorge Serrano, was president of Guatemala from 1991 to 1993. Robertson had this to say about Serrano: "Serrano continues the enlightened leadership of his patron, former President Rios Montt, who insisted on honesty in government and then had every key official sign a pledge that read, "I will not steal; I will not lie; I will not abuse." But in contrast, Amnesty International said the following about Rios Montt's leadership:

> "In just the four months of Gen. Rios Montt's rule, Amnesty International had documented more than 2,000 extrajudicial killings attributed to the Guatemalan army. Furthermore, these killings were done in horrible ways: people of all ages were not only shot to death, they were burned alive, hacked to death, disemboweled, drowned, beheaded. Small children were smashed against rocks or bayoneted to death.⁹"

Robertson's relationship with Frederick Chiluba is no less interesting than his other murderous friends. Chiluba was the President of Zambia from 1991 to 2002. Chiluba declared Zambia's commitment to become a Christian country during his rule. Previously public schools became Christian-only, even though Zambia has a fairly large minority of Muslims and Hindus. Non-Christian concerns about lack of schools for their children were met with Chiluba's solution for them to open their own schools. Since dissension is not particularly wise within a dictatorial society, the national television and radio stations conformed to Christian programming. In an interview with Chiluba on the 700 Club in 1995, Robertson told him, "Your country is not only the standard for Africa but for the rest of the world." Afterward, he asked his audience, "Wouldn't you love to have someone like that as President of the United States of America?" Robertson is even skilled in exploiting the exploiters. Robertson's greed, fanaticism and theocratic goals have led him into acquaintances with a strange bunch.[10]

"Racism"

Is the Christian Coalition a racist group? The following quotes and some excerpts attributed to Richard Benedetto appeared in *USA Today*.

Eugene Rivers, a black evangelical minister accused the Christian Coalition of being a "racist organization" because of its nearly all-white membership, their strict conservative views, and its "failure" to reach out to black churches. This accusation came as a group of eleven white and black evangelical leaders held a news conference to offer an alternative voice to the increasingly vocal religious right, which they say "does not speak for all the faithful."

"It certainly does not speak for twenty-three million black Christians, nor does it speak for all white Christians. It only speaks for itself," said Jim Wallis, pastor of Sojourners Community Church in Washington, DC.

Eugene Rivers, pastor of Azusa Christian Community Church in Boston, said the Christian Coalition "has its roots in the same [white] political forces that opposed Martin Luther King." He also stated that "it seeks to appeal to a Southern white male base that over the last thirty years has been hostile to the advances of blacks."

This charge was immediately denied as "untrue" by coalition spokesman Mike Russell, who stated that his group is continuously reaching out to black Christians. I wonder if God recognizes or distinguishes between "black" Christians or "white" Christians, or just Christians. Russell, when asked about membership, could not offer an estimate of black membership other than to say it is "small." He expatiated, "We're a predominantly white group, that's obvious, but we're committed to making inroads into the black community. It's a huge area for growth potential for us," Russell said.

Founded in 1990 by Pat Robertson, the Christian Coalition has grown to 1.6 million members, more than a twenty-five million dollar budget and a muscular presence on Capitol Hill. I wonder how much of donated funds are allocated to buy votes on Capitol Hill.

"The alternative to the religious right is not the religious left," said Wallis. "We need a politics whose values are more spiritual than ideological—a politics rooted in civility, compassion and community."

"Beware of political parties and foreign alliances."
—George Washington

CHAPTER 3

MORAL MAJORITY

*"No man can serve two masters: for either he will hate
the one, and love the other; or else he will hold to
the one, and despise the other.
You cannot serve God and mammon."*
—Matthew 6:24

"The Falwell Empire"

Jerry Falwell is senior pastor at the seventeen thousand member Thomas Road Baptist Church in Lynchburg, Virginia. The membership rises or falls with university student enrollment. Falwell heads the Old Time Gospel Hour Network syndicated on dozens of cable channels and is the Chancellor of Liberty University. He used his television clout to propel the Moral Majority—a right wing conservative political group. Recently, he launched the Liberty Federation, whose involvement with foreign affairs has launched it into national and world prominence.

Dr. Falwell receives $237,000 yearly from the university, plus a salary from the church and several hundred thousand for tape royalties and speaking engagements. He also collects revenue on rental properties and a percentage of profits from businesses outside the church, usually registered in the name of his wife or one of their three children. Besides hundreds of gifts for birthdays, anniversaries, Christmas and good-old-boy gifts, he receives free housing, cars, and miscellaneous living expenses. The church furnishes Falwell with a private jet and pilot for vacations and speaking engagements while twenty-four-hour police protection is provided by the university. The Jerry Falwell family proper owns a private airport, a road paving and heavy equipment company, a shopping mall, and a video duplicating company. And for all of this Falwell says: "I am only a servant working for God."

Television evangelist Jerry Falwell founded the Moral Majority in 1979, an organization of the conservative religious right. The Moral Majority functions as a coalition that lobbies for such causes as school prayer and anti-abortion legislation. This religious coalition was built and grown on the premise that America is basically moral and that the majority of her people desire honest change and good government. Since its conception in the late 1970s, however, the Moral Majority has proven the opposite, even among Falwell's own rank-and-file.

"Another aspect of Falwell's crusade has received less attention but is at least as important in its implications. He is mobilizing and altering the consciousness of that once insular component of American religion, known as fundamentalism."[11] Falwell is proposing a so-called 'neo-fundamentalism,' designed to give the 'new right' groups more political power. The 'new right' comprises the religious elite. The Moral Majority and Christian Voice, two of the largest politically active groups were organized to be pro-family, pro-life, pro-God, pro-American, and mostly, pro-pocketbook. They played a major role and claimed victory in electing Ronald Reagan as President while ousting several liberal senators in the same election.

Basically, there is nothing wrong with such organizations seeking democratic goals and working for the good of all concerned. However, as in most institutions, a few key individuals usually manipulate the internal structure, force biased opinions, and develop their own dictatorship. Even conservative religious people are human and wrestle constantly with sin and pride. Sin and pride almost always win.

The largest percentage of Moral Majority and Christian Voice folks are, in essence only, members of the "new morality" group. New morality represents a group of religious people with a humanistic view that reflects that adultery is free love, stealing is the misappropriation of funds, and a philosophy of "it's my life and I will do as I please." The group comprises the church people who are pro-life and pro-God on Sunday and usually pro-

Satan the rest of the week. Our modern day "born again" crowd can be likened to the religious Pharisees that led Jesus to call "a generation of vipers" (Matt. 3:7). These religious fanatics eventually crucified Him at Calvary.

There are over half a million members in the clergy of the United States. Inevitably, many fall to alcoholism, get entangled in liaisons, siphon off church money, and nearly thirty percent fail in marriage. In fact, Jerry Falwell's own daughter's marriage ended in divorce.

Questions of sexual misconduct in past years have affected the careers of leading figures in mainline Protestantism—Jimmy Swaggart and Jim Bakker in particular. The Roman Catholic bishops' conference recently acknowledged an increase in reported incidents of sexual abuse of children by catholic priests, and drinking and drunkenness has been on the rise for over three decades. Bishops in a number of dioceses, for example, have been accused of responding to reports of pedophilia by quietly transferring priests without notifying the proper authorities or actively monitoring their rehabilitation efforts.

How does all this fit into Falwell's Moral Majority? Is this a misnomer? Falwell is convinced that God is calling millions of Americans from the so-called "Silent Majority"[12] to join the Moral Majority and turn America around. I believe, however, that ministers of the Bible acting as shepherds of the flock should, indeed, spend more time in pursuit of this vocation. Politics and issues have no place in the pulpit or in the church as a whole.

By the way, whatever happened to the mailing list of the Moral Majority that my name was on when it was dissolved in the late 1980s? It was sold for fifty-thousand dollars by Jonathan Falwell, Jerry's second son and heir apparent to the empire. Now, is this wrong? No, because mailing lists are sold all the time. Is this unethical? Yes, because it only substantiates my theses that religion is being sold and great profits are made by religious leaders. When the news media attempted to interview Jonathan Falwell, he had taken a palpable big game hunting expedition in Alaska. In my opinion, he got the big game before leaving for Alaska.

> *"Even so you also outwardly appear righteous unto men,*
> *but within you are full of hypocrisy and iniquity."*
> —Matthew 23:38

"Falwell vs. Clinton"

"I exhort therefore, that, first of all, supplications, prayers, intercessions, and giving of thanks, be made for all men; for kings, and for all that are in authority; that we may lead a quiet and peaceable life in all godliness and honesty. For this is good and acceptable in the sight of God our Saviour."

—I Timothy 2:1-3

The office of the President deserves and demands respect. It is not a question of whether we agree or disagree, it is a command from God to honor those in authority. Former President Bill Clinton, like a lot of us, probably has some skeletons in his closet. However, his position required the highest esteem. Our dear brother Jerry Falwell needs to learn this lesson well. His own closet is probably not entirely free from skeletons either.

Falwell's personality is courteous and well mannered; he is a hard man not to like. But some of his actions as a man and as a minister are very questionable.

"Specifically, in his zeal to raise money for his ministry, I believe he has sometimes overstepped the bounds of good taste and Christian charity. At no time has that been more evident than in his offer of videos that accuse Bill and Hillary Clinton of a variety of sins, from adultery to murder, and in his refusal to let a Clinton supporter respond to the charges on Falwell's television program."[13]

In 1992, the Old-Time Gospel Hour and Christian Action Network aired commercials showing excerpts from the videos that accused President Clinton and the First Lady of sordid indiscretions and crimes ranging from adultery to murder. Sources in the video imputed Clinton of having a hand in mysterious plane crashes, fires, break-ins, and murders that victimized people who were collecting damaging information about the President.

Falwell sold about forty thousand Clinton videos for about forty dollars each, according to Mark DeMoss, a spokesman and valet for Falwell. Figures prove that the video sales would bring about 1.6 million dollars. DeMoss believed that all the money went to the cost of advertising, royalties, and various other expenses.

"As far as I know, that offer did not make any money," DeMoss said. "Expenses include buying air time to promote the tapes and paying a royalty to Citizens for Honest Government, a California-based grassroots group that produced the videos." Continuing, DeMoss stated, "Whether the royalty was a couple of bucks, five or ten dollars per video, I honestly don't know. I don't know if I would tell you if I did know."[14]

For example, let us say that a blank tape costs two dollars and that a royalty fee costs ten dollars. The vast majority of air time on the television was already paid for through gifts from faith partners and friends of Liberty University. Thus, we have a twelve dollar expense on a forty dollar tape, which leaves a profit of roughly 1.1 million dollars. Sources close to Falwell say they do not know where the money went or they won't say. Dave Schleck, staff writer who interviewed DeMoss does not know where the profits went either.

I believe that a guarded secret around Liberty University and Lynchburg, Virginia, if revealed, will divulge where some of the profits went. The Falwell family owns and operates a company called TransAmerica Video. It was opened in the 1980s as TransAmerica Duplicators, Inc. This company, independent of The Old Time Gospel Hour and Liberty University, makes tapes under the direction of Jerry Falwell. They are advertised and sold on the television network. The owner of TransAmerica is Jonathan Falwell, also co-pastor of Thomas Road Baptist Church. The company was the one responsible for selling the Moral Majority mailing list. Even though it is greatly denied, Christians love and covet money like anyone else. The proof is in the pudding.

Direct criticism from the White House did not impede or make Falwell slow down. President Clinton lashed out against the video during a highly publicized radio interview from Air Force One. Falwell was unfazed and only months later, started marketing a second video, "Clinton Chronicles."

Is Bill Clinton guilty of adultery? The question was brought up before the election, but voters decided to reelect him anyway. They concluded that he, his wife, and his God, not Jerry Falwell, was to judge that particular sin.

Is Clinton guilty of conspiring to murder his political enemies or those who might politically embarrass him? Why, nobody in their right mind believes that and there have been no great national news stories on that subject because, to date, no credible evidence exists to suggest even a microbe of truth to the charges. This also includes the evidence on the tapes Falwell has sold.

Recently, Falwell has acknowledged that he does not have any evidence to back up the charges on the tapes. He states, "The videos represent a legitimate news story that has been overlooked by the liberal Clinton-loving media, and that the American people deserve a chance to see and hear an unexpurgated recitation of these charges."[15] This means, in simple terms, that someone made money by shading the truth about President Clinton.

A federal judge in Roanoke, Virginia, ruled in March of 1995 on whether Christian Action Network (CAN) violated federal laws with its 1992 commercial that attacked Bill Clinton. The ruling favored CAN and Falwell by stating that the First Amendment guarantees Americans free speech with only minimal restrictions.

Christian Action Network is supposedly a nonprofit organization started by Martin Mawyer, a former Moral Majority employee of Falwell's. In the past, it has raised two million dollars or more yearly and supports a full-time Capitol Hill lobbyist.

Now, here is the question. Is this a free-speech issue or a tax issue? Are our taxes subsidizing certain nonprofit organizations to make partisan attacks on the people of their choice? Religious organizations certainly need more accountability. They continue to "fleece the sheep" and waste huge amounts of money from honest people. God help them!

> *"These six things doth the Lord hate; yes, seven are an abomination unto him: a proud look, a lying tongue, and hands that shed innocent blood, a heart that deviseth wicked imaginations, feet that be swift in running to mischief, a false witness that speaketh lies, and he that soweth discord among brethren."*
> —Proverbs 6:16-19

CHAPTER 4

ORBIS UNUM

Jesus said; "I will build my church…" (Matt. 16:18). Pat Robertson, Rick Warren, Brian McLaren, and other neo-evangelicals believe you can build God's church through power, money—your money—and their version of humanistic criteria and values.

Through the last two thousand years there have been religious groups competing for the "upper-hand" to dominate the masses, and of course, the economy in our world. The Holy Crusades sought to wipe out the infidel—now Christians are the infidels—with the use of the sword. Thus, religious killing is definitely not something new in today's world. Secret religious societies of the last two millennia have sought dominance in the name of Christ. The Knights Templars—legendary protectors of the Holy Grail—were the first. Then came the Freemasons, and more recently, the Illuminati of the last two-hundred years.

Today we have a "new order" on the horizon being formed by the groups calling themselves "the neo-fundamentalists." The "Orbis Unum" or "One World" church is now being established through secret societies and religious alliances around the world. This hoard of "religious conservatives" is the same ones voting for George Bush, Dick Cheney, and for wars we cannot win. They have turned from the Bible and towards humanistic psychology; all counter-productive to the cause of Christ. It is well known that it takes money to run the train and this "new world order" is definitely money driven.

"Word-Faith Movement"

The following has been excerpted from an article titled "The Word of Faith Movement," in April 1999 by Pastor Gary Gilley of the Southern View Chapel in Springfield, Illinois.

The fastest growing segment of professing Christianity today is the "Word-Faith Movement," also known as "The Positive Confession" or simply "Faith Movement." Its growth is at least partially due to the massive amounts of money the leaders are able to extract from the faithful. This influx of cash allows for huge buildings and extensive ministries, and more importantly, wide exposure on television, which translates into large increases in memberships. Well known personalities within this movement include Kenneth Hagin, Kenneth Copeland, Robert Tilton, Yonggi Cho, Benny Hinn, Marilyn Hickey, Frederick Price, John Avanzin, Charles Capps, Jerry Savelle, Morris Cerullo, and of course Paul and Jan Crouch of The Trinity Broadcasting Network (TBN).

This alliance spreads worldwide. For example, Yonggi Cho is a member and he pastors the 700,000 Full Gospel Yoido Church in South Korea. He is a renowned speaker in the U.S. and at conferences around the world.

The "Faith Movement" is a theology that appeals to the masses because man is in control; God gave Adam dominion, and thus, He no longer has dominion. This false teaching gives man certain qualities that are synonymous with a deity. God becomes the servant of man and is now required to give man whatever he asks in faith. This "name-it, claim-it" theology of prosperity is immoral and ungodly. It is inherently self serving and egotistical because it teaches that by simply naming something desired, God is obligated to provide it. The Word Faith 'name-it, claim-it' philosophy makes God like a genie in a bottle whose purpose becomes to serve man for his glory; not the other way around. It all comes back to another church legalism that makes congregants' minds fertile ground for get rich quick schemes.

"CUFI"

Christians United for Israel (CUFI) is represented by more than thirty million evangelical fundamentalist Christians in the United States. The pro-Israel lobby has three primary aims: (1) unite Christian supporters of Israel, to speak with one voice, (2) establish a "rapid response" capability to flood Capitol Hill with various modes of correspondence at short notice on issues of concern to Israel; and (3) organize "Night to Honor Israel" events in every major city in the US.[16] Some of the leaders supporting CUFI include John Hagee, Matt Crouch, Jack Hanford, Paul Walker, assistant general and overseer of the Church of God denomination, Pastor Rod Parsley, Benny Hinn, Kenneth Copeland, and Gary Bauer, president of the Family Research Council—the Washington, DC-based lobbying arm of James Dobson's "Focus on the Family." According to Hagee Christian leadership must join forces to move as one body to respond to the crisis that Israel will be facing in the future. Leading Baptist preacher Jerry Falwell has been added to the CUFI list because John Hagee, televangelist of Cornerstone Church in San Antonio, Texas, and Pat Robertson have converted Falwell to a belief in what Christians refer to as "dual covenant theology."[17] Basically this means that Jews, who, as a religion, do not believe that Jesus is the Messiah. However, their dual covenant theology says Jews don't need to believe in Jesus as the Messiah to go to heaven. They can now go to heaven in their own special way.

Boy O' Boy! Isn't it great to know that all that is necessary to achieve heaven is for one of our infamous conservative religious leaders to come up with a new theology? This is especially comforting when evangelist Pat Robertson wanted a U.S. "hit team" to assassinate President Chavez of Venezuela. We can classify this as Pat Robertson's "save some, kill some" theology.

Always remember, according to 2nd Timothy, Chapter 3, in the last days, high-minded men and women will come. These are lovers of pleasures more than lovers of God; having a form of godliness, but denying the power thereof: from such turn away.

"The Purpose Driven Life"

Rick Warren's latest book entitled *The Purpose Driven Life* is a sequel to his book, *The Purpose Driven Church*. These two books rank second in sales only to the Holy Bible itself. Warren says, "The goal of *The Purpose Driven Life* is to help people develop a heart for the world." However, many believe the title of these books should be "The Purpose Driven Lie" or "Porpoise Driven Life," because of the new-age and humanistic philosophy entwined throughout the teachings. There is also a great deal of psychological manipulation that fuels today's church growth movement.

Rick Warren has teamed up with "new-age" guru, Ken Blanchard to train one billion people by the year 2020. These are to be the foot soldiers of the future instructed in the New Age mysticism and taught how to go into altered states of consciousness. Several South African presidents have already aligned with Rick Warren's philosophies and will be the launching pad into Asia and Europe. Initially, fifty-five million dollars is now being raised to get started. This "One World" movement along with the Christian *or* evangelical fundamentalists is no more than an occult designed to control world religions.

The following article, "The Adulation of Man in The Purpose Driven Life" by Richard Bennett explains the fallacies of this new movement. It is printed in its entirety with permission of the author.[18]

Rick Warren's *The Purpose-Driven Life* is more than a bestseller, it's become a movement. In the words of the author himself his megachurch program is "Revival awakening or miracle...Over twelve thousand churches from all fifty states and nineteen countries have now participated in 40 Days of Purpose. Many of these churches have reported that it was the most transforming event in their congregation's history." Rick is also the founder of Pastors.com, a global Internet community that serves and mentors those in ministry worldwide. Over 60,000 pastors subscribe to Rick Warren's Ministry Toolbox." On this Webpage he states,

"Our Purpose is to encourage pastors, ministers, and church leaders with tools and resources for growing healthy churches...Every resource you purchase helps provide free resources to the 1.5 million pastors and lay pastors in third world countries. God has allowed us through your support to reach over different countries on all seven continents."

The movement is becoming a global empire. Warren asserts, "God is a global God...Much of world already thinks globally. The largest media and business conglomerates are all multinational...Get a globe or map and pray for nations by name. The Bible says, 'If you ask me, I will give you the nations; all the people on earth will be yours.'" (Warren, however, has overlooked the fact that this promise was made uniquely to Christ Jesus, and not to megachurches seeking expansion).

Even the business world is looking on with awe. Forbes.com in an article called "Christian Capitalism Megachurches, Megabusinesses" acknowledged that,

"Maybe churches aren't so different from corporations...Pastor Rick Warren, who founded Saddleback Church in Lake Forest, Calif., in 1980, has deftly used technology as well as marketing to spread his message...No doubt, churches have learned some valuable lessons from corporations. Now maybe they can teach businesses a thing or two. Companies would certainly appreciate having the armies of non-paid, loyal volunteers."

The empire of influence of which Warren boasts is echoed by thousands of pastors and Christian leaders around the world. At least eighteen million copies of his book have been sold since its release in September 2002. It is now selling in many translations. Literally thousands of churches have used the book and the materials that accompany it during special campaigns called 40 Days of Purpose. The book is divided into forty chapters purporting to explain in 40 days the five purposes of one's life. Indeed, the thesis of the book is found on p. 136,

> "He [God] created the church to meet your five deepest needs: a purpose to live for, people to live with, principles to live by, a profession to live out, and power to live on. There is no other place on earth where you can find all five of these benefits in one place."

Warren is dead wrong in his list of "deepest needs". On the authority of the Bible, the first and foremost need of any man is perfect righteousness before the All Holy God. It is Christ Jesus' righteousness alone that God will accept as a propitiation for any man's sin and sin nature. This primary need of man is constantly shown in the Bible but Warren does not even mention this foundational truth in his list of "deepest needs". Warren's quick switch from God's purpose to man's methods falls under the first temptation ever recorded in the Bible. Satan offered to Eve the fruit as the way of achieving a spiritual purpose, "in the day ye eat thereof, then your eyes shall be opened and ye shall be as gods, knowing good and evil." Warren teaches that God "created the church to meet your five deepest needs" just as the Roman Catholic Church says,

> "The Church is the mother of all believers." Warren, like Rome, has switched from obedience to the Word and Person of the Living God to submission to a church to achieve one's needs. It is the oldest and cleverest temptation known to man.

Warren's gospel, the root flaw

The Apostle Paul showed the need for the Gospel by the fact that the whole world is guilty before God. He declared, "now we know that what things so ever the law saith, it saith to them who are under the law: that every mouth may be stopped, and all the world may become guilty before God." All are "by nature children of wrath", guilty before the all Holy God. To appear before Him, therefore, each needs a perfect righteousness. James summarizes the whole condition of man when he says, "for whosoever shall keep the whole law, and yet offend in one point, he is guilty of all." Guilt before God shows the need for the Gospel and as such is the basis for the Gospel. Conviction of sin by the Holy Spirit drives the sinner to trust truly on Christ Jesus alone, as the publican in the parable of the Lord cried out, "God be merciful to me a sinner." With Warren, this conviction of guilt is reduced by psychological terminology to the condition of "unconsciously punishing of oneself". He states,

> "Many people are driven by guilt…Guilt-driven people are manipulated by memories. They allow their past to control their future. They often unconsciously punish themselves by sabotaging their own success. When Cain sinned, his guilt disconnected him from God's presence, and God said, 'You will be a restless wanderer on the earth.' That describes most people today—wandering through life without a purpose.

Rather than sin being shown to be an evil of infinite significance because it is committed against an infinite Person, Warren's pop psychology defines sin as acts of people "sabotaging their own success." He continues,

> "God won't ask about your religious background or doctrinal views. The only thing that will matter is, did you accept what Jesus did for you and did you learn to love and trust him?"

> "If you learn to love and trust God's Son, Jesus, you will be invited to spend the rest of eternity with him. On the other hand, if you reject his love, forgiveness, and salvation, you will spend eternity apart from God forever."

Biblically speaking, it is absolute folly to tell an unconvicted sinner merely to "learn to love and trust God's Son, Jesus". No one can be saved without recognition of his own sin personally against Holy God, and without turning away from that sin. So while it is true that the only thing that matters "is to learn to love and trust Him", this love and trust is impossible unless the Holy Spirit has convicted a person that he is a depraved sinner without any hope in himself. Warren does endeavor to define sin when he states,

> All sin, at its root, is failing to give God glory. It is loving anything else more than God. Refusing to bring glory to God is prideful rebellion, and it is the sin that caused Satan's fall—and ours, too. In different ways we all lived for our own glory, not God's. The Bible says, 'All have sinned and fall short of the glory of God.'"

While this is true, Warren still has not acknowledged personal guilt and personal need for Christ's perfect righteousness and perfect sacrifice. Warren's persistent declarations one's "self worth" and "true self", as we will shortly document, totally negates what he says about "prideful rebellion". The book and movement, on the contrary, major in upholding "self worth" and "true self" thus endorsing the very "prideful rebellion" it states the cause of our fall, even as it was Satan's. This type of a contradictory statement made by Warren makes it difficult to analyze the book. While this is so, it is all the more necessary to do such an analysis. Without the Apostle Paul's conviction, "I know that in me (that is, in my flesh,) dwelleth no good thing," there can be no true faith in Christ Jesus, nor even a growth in sanctification before God. The first key flaw in the Warren's gospel message is the negation of the very basis needed for salvation. As the Lord Himself proclaimed, "they that are whole have no need of the physician, but they that are sick: I came not to call the righteous, but sinners to repentance."

The heart of Warren's gospel

Warren's gospel message gets worse as he proceeds in the book. He assures his readers,

"Real life begins by committing yourself completely to Jesus Christ. If you are not sure you have done this, all you need to do is receive and believe. The Bible promises, 'To all who received him, to those who believed in his name, he gave the right to become children of God.' Will you accept God's offer?"

What Warren has neglected in his teaching of John 1:12 is that the following verse, verse thirteen, explains how a person is born again, "which were born, not of blood, nor of the will of the flesh, nor of the will of man, but of God." Warren has completely ignored the fact that to receive and believe is not of the will of man, but of God. It is the grace of God that makes a person willing to believe, for the heart is changed by God's power alone. To leave out this essential point changes the focus from God to man. Such a change of focus from God to man is lethal to salvation because there is no power within man to change himself. This grace must come from God. If, however, Warren had taught his readers to look to God for His grace, he would not have a ready-made message that is marketable. For Warren it is advantageous to leave out "not of blood, nor of the will of the flesh, nor of the will of man, but of God". In leaving out this essential factor of the Gospel he can in fact propose that which this verse of Scripture rules out! The Lord is consistent in His Word, "I will have mercy on whom I will have mercy, and I will have compassion on whom I will have compassion. So then it is not of him that willeth, nor of him that runneth, but of God that sheweth mercy." Eternal life is bestowed on a person not because man begins the work, but it is because God gives salvation out of His mercy and grace. Such is the written purpose of God. Warren's written purpose is the opposite. It begins, he says, with man, "Real life begins by committing yourself..." But this is a deception for which Warren will have to pay before the All Holy God. "Be not deceived; God is not mocked...It is a fearful thing to fall into the hands of the living God." The power and dread of God's vindictive wrath is great. There will be eternal misery for those who teach a false gospel, their punishment shall come from God's own hand.

Warren progresses in his bogus gospel message,

> "First, believe. Believe God loves you and made you for his purposes. Believe you're not an accident. Believe you were made to last forever. Believe God has chosen you to have a relationship with Jesus, who died on the cross for you. Believe that no matter what you've done, God wants to forgive you.
>
> "Second, receive. Receive Jesus into your life as Lord and Savior. Receive his forgiveness for your sins. Receive his Spirit, who will give you the power to fulfill your life purpose. Wherever you are reading this, I invite you to bow your head and quietly whisper the prayer that will change your eternity: 'Jesus, I believe in you and I receive you.' Go ahead. "If you sincerely meant that prayer, congratulations! Welcome to the family of God!"

According to Warren's teaching, it is the prayer that one whispers that changes a person for eternity. Instead of magnifying the enormity of sin and setting forth its eternal consequences, Warren says, "Believe that no matter what you've done, God wants to forgive you." With one sweet lie he attempts to wipe out all the teaching of the prophets in the Old Testament and the Lord Christ Jesus and the Apostles in the consistent teaching on the abhorrence of sin and the need of repentance. In place of the Gospel as "the power of God unto salvation" "in which the righteousness of God revealed from faith to faith," Warren merely gives a whispered prayer. It is difficult to envisage a greater insult to Christ Jesus, whose perfect life and perfect sacrifice are the basis of genuine salvation.

The Apostle Paul declares that the righteousness of God is manifested, "But now the righteousness of God without the law is manifested, being witnessed by the law and the prophets." Before God, sin had to be punished and true righteousness established. God's holiness demanded the perfect life and perfect sacrifice of Christ Jesus to satisfy His wrath against sin. But for Warren, as we had seen, sin is said to be "sabotaging...success" so the whole concept of perfect righteousness being manifested before God is totally missing. With the omission goes the omission of the concept of grace as the means of obtaining that perfect righteousness. According to Warren's doctrine, salvation is "bow your head and quietly whisper the prayer that will change your eternity." In Scripture, salvation is God's action based on Christ's finished work on the cross that is credited to the true believer, "being justified freely by His grace through the redemption that is in Christ Jesus." God's direct action shows His grace so that our eyes are fixed on Him in faith. Understanding Warren's bogus gospel, and outrageously presumptuous "welcome to the family of God", we can but repeat the words of the Lord, "woe unto you…for ye shut up the kingdom of heaven against men." By a false gospel and false assurance of admittance into the family of God, Warren has excluded further seeking for the truth, "woe unto you…for ye have taken away the key of knowledge." The Gospel, in which the finished work of the Lord is proclaimed, is such that it cannot be changed by a lie that ignores repentance and adds a whispered prayer that insults the meaning and application of redemption. This replacement of Warren's purpose for God's purpose has dreadful consequences: "though we, or an angel from heaven, preach any other gospel unto you than that which we have preached unto you, let him be accursed." Christ Jesus the Lord and His Gospel cannot be insulted with impunity. As the receiver of stolen goods is as accountable as the thief, so one who promotes such a pretended gospel is as accountable in the sight of God as the impostor himself.

Self worth: The glorification of man

Basic to Warren's program is the strong appeal of promised instantaneous results in the enhancement of one's imaginations of his own self worth. What is completely ignored is the solemn fact that by nature man is a fallen creature, alienated from the life of God, dead in trespasses and sins, and that his only hope is outside of himself and in Christ Jesus alone. Although Warren states that the book is "not about you," the main focus is persistently on building up one's "self worth". He continually appeals to the reader's self-interests. The following are some examples,

"The way you see your life shapes your life. How you define life determines your destiny."

"You are a bundle of incredible abilities, an amazing creation of God. Part of the church's responsibility is to identify and release your abilities for serving God."

"The best use of your life is to serve God out of your shape. To do this you must discover your shape, learn to accept and enjoy it, and then develop it to its fullest potential."

This equates exactly with the Hinduism in its teaching, "By understanding your true Self, by coming to know one's own undying soul, one then arrives at the knowledge of Brahman itself..." While Warren's teaching is comparable with Hinduism, the most likely source of Warren's teaching is Carl Jung. Discovering one's "power of the inner voice" or one's fullest potential is what Jung taught, "Only the man who can consciously assent to the power of the inner voice becomes a personality." What is much more serious is that Warren's teaching has the same basic premise as Roman Catholicism. The Vatican's official foundational starting point is man himself. Rome states,

"It is man himself who must be saved: it is mankind that must be renewed. It is man, therefore, who is the key to this discussion, man considered whole and entire, with body and soul, heart and conscience, mind and will. This is the reason why this sacred Synod, in proclaiming the noble destiny of man and affirming an element of the divine in him, offers to co-operate unreservedly with mankind in fostering a sense of brotherhood to correspond to this destiny of theirs."

"Discovering one's shape[,] accepting and enjoy[ing] it[,] developing it to its fullest potential" is same basic foundation as the Church of Rome and Hinduism have, as we have already seen, but the same is true also of Islam and Buddhism—all of them have for their focal point the basic goodness of mankind. Warren summarizes this basic foundation in the following words,

> "If you are that important to God, and he considers you valuable enough to keep with him for eternity, what greater significance could you have?

The Scriptures, however, depict no such value or goodness within man. Rather the Holy Spirit teaches that "the heart is deceitful above all things, and desperately wicked, who can know it?" "Thus saith the LORD; Cursed be the man that trusteth in man, and maketh flesh his arm, and whose heart departeth from the LORD."

Warren even goes so far as to distort a Scripture text to uphold his treasured concept of "true self." He states, "The Bible says, 'Self-help is no help at all. Self-sacrifice is the way, my way, to finding yourself, your true self'". The passage he quotes is a contrived paraphrase of Matthew 16:25 from The Message. The Lord in fact said, "For whosoever will save his life shall lose it: and whosoever will lose his life for my sake shall find it." The Lord clearly taught that we are to consider our lives dead in order to follow Him. This passage does not teach anything about "true self" or self esteem. Warren used the counterfeit paraphrase to fantasize that the Lord had spoken of "finding yourself, your true self". The craze of finding your "true self", one of the hallmarks of the 1960's hippy crowd, has now made its mark in this popularized debasing of Christianity.

Self-exaltation "salvation" is worthless

This same glorification of man Warren teaches in many different ways.

> "You only bring him [God] enjoyment by being you. Anytime you reject any part of yourself, you are rejecting God's wisdom and sovereignty in creating you."

> "When you are sleeping, God gazes at you with love, because you were his idea. He loves you as if you were the only person on earth."

But Warren does not stop here with his adulation of man. The height of his glorification of man is found in the statement that makes the personal worth of the reader the purpose of Christ's death on the cross. In doing so, "self-worth" is pushed to the point not only of perverting the Gospel but also of insulting the Lord Himself. Warren states,

> "If you want to know how much you matter to God, look at Christ with his arms outstretched on the cross, saying, 'I love you this much! I'd rather die than live without you.'".

These words "I'd rather die than live without you" are part of a lyric of the "backstreet boys." These words, put into the mouth of the Lord Christ Jesus by Warren, are a blasphemy. Christ Jesus the God-man, does not have a love that is dependant on man. If he had such a dependency, He would not be God. To teach that the love of the Lord Jesus Christ is unholy, as Warren has, is both an insult and irreverence. It exalts sinful man to a position of control regarding the eternal Son of God. Can such an imagination be anything other than profanity? "He opened his mouth in blasphemy against God, to blaspheme his name."

In Scripture, Christ's love and sacrifice were to demonstrate that God is "just and the justifier of him which believeth in Jesus." Nevertheless, Warren's doctrine makes living with sinful man the centerpiece of God's purpose. In Scripture, the focus of God's purpose was the demonstration of His justice and holiness in the Person and sacrifice of Christ Jesus. Sinful man was included in this great manifestation of the righteousness of God as a recipient by grace of the redemption paid. Warren's grandiose glorification of sinful man to the extent that Christ Jesus would rather die than to live without him totally reverses the biblical message that God does all for His own glory. All is of Him and from Him, and therefore all is to Him and for Him. He made all creation according to His will and for His praise. The Lord God Almighty's purpose exposes the ridicule, vainglory and even blasphemy of Rick Warren.

Fallen man is depraved in every part of his nature and being, and it is not within his power to undo his depravity, to save himself or rescue himself. To try to aggrandize the fallen man, as Warren does, is futile because there is no moral salvation in man's worth. A person's only hope lies outside of himself, in divine worth and power. Human nature as such is dead in trespasses and sins. Water cannot flow uphill, nor can the natural man act contrary to his corrupt nature.

All human beings are destitute of the principles and powers of spiritual life. They are cut off from God, the fountain of life. They are spiritually dead as a condemned criminal is said to be a dead man. Thus the Lord Christ Jesus declared, "for from within, out of the heart of men, proceed evil thoughts, adulteries, fornications, murders, thefts, covetousness, wickedness, deceit, lasciviousness, an evil eye, blasphemy, pride, foolishness, all these evil things come from within, and defile the man." Christ declared, "That which is born of the flesh is flesh." He signified that that which is propagated by fallen man is depraved. If the principle of self-worth and the ability to choose Christ were true, the conclusion would inevitably follow that those who used their ability to choose Christ could lawfully boast of their active participation in their salvation. But the truth is that faith itself is God's gift, "for by grace are you saved through faith; and that not of yourselves: it is the gift of God: Not of works, lest any man should boast." Until one realizes his personal condition of being spiritually dead before the All Holy God, one will never properly appreciate God's grace. Salvation begins not in self worth and self-movement but by divine power. Scripture is utterly clear on this matter: "Of his own will begat he us with the word of truth."

"For it is God which works in you both to will and to do of his good pleasure." God gives life to the spiritually dead will of man by giving His grace. It is the power of the Holy Spirit that overcomes the pride of the natural man, so that one is ready to come to Christ to receive life. In the Lord's own words, "the hour is coming, and now is, when the dead shall hear the voice of the Son of God: and they that hear shall live." As the Lord also explained, "It is written in the prophets, and they shall be all taught of God. Every man therefore that has heard, and has learned of the Father, comes unto me."

"Self-salvation" promoted on the basis of human worth and dignity is ingrained in human nature. It is found in all man-made religions. It is pivotal to the message of Warren's book and movement. Warren's teachings deny the biblical truth that man is totally depraved. Subsequently, he denies the absolute necessity of God's grace. The relationship between spiritual death and grace is graphically given in Scripture, "that as sin has reigned unto death, even so might grace reign through righteousness unto eternal life by Jesus Christ our Lord." Without understanding the total depravity of those to whom the Gospel is given, the Gospel will remain a dead letter. In leaving out the biblical truth that "there is none righteous, no, not one" and substituting for it the self-worth of man, Warren's arrogance has reached a level predicted in the Scripture, "I will ascend above the heights of the clouds; I will be like the most High."

Conclusion

Now that we have documented that a bogus gospel message is given in the 40 Days of Purpose in *The Purpose-Driven Life* we are obliged to "earnestly contend for the faith which was once delivered unto the saints," and to "stand fast in one spirit, with one mind striving together for the faith of the gospel." Through the Warren movement, multitudes are being deceived on the very meaning of the Gospel of salvation. Vast numbers sincerely believe that they have received Christ as their personal Savior while in fact all that they have received into their right hand is a man-made ritual and "covenant" commitment to a church, which they have obligated themselves by vow to fulfill. While many of the articles regarding Warren commend the good things Warren has had to say, they forget that the Lord Himself and His Apostles utterly condemned the presentation of a false gospel. How can we expect any true revival and the bringing of the everlasting righteousness of Christ Jesus into the lives of men and women, if we are not willing to expose pretensions of him who embraces a "christ" unknown in the pages of Scripture, who presents a sham gospel and who is willing to commend the devotees of the apostate system of Rome? He is a deceiver who willfully defrauds, after all the light of the Gospel of grace has been clearly set forth. It must not be thought strange that there are deceivers of the Lord Christ's name and dignity now, for there were such of old, even in the Apostles' times. The danger and evil of departure from the true Gospel is in effect and reality a departure from God Himself. "Whosoever transgresseth, and abideth not in the doctrine of Christ, hath not God. He that abideth in the doctrine of Christ, he hath both the Father and the Son."

CHAPTER 5

FIRST AMENDMENT

Congress shall make no law respecting an establishment of religion, or prohibiting the free exercise thereof; or abridging the freedom of speech, or of the press; or the right of the people peaceably to assemble, and to petition the Government for a redress of grievances.

—1st Amendment

This great nation was founded and preserved by such words that have depth and ring true. Brave men and women, for the fulfillment of this cause, sacrificed their time, wealth, and their lives when called upon to do so, in order to preserve this young nation. Today, many individuals are using the First Amendment and the freedom that we hold dear to advance their own causes. I do not know of one single televangelist or any of their children who fought for this country, although many of them are "prowar." They are very patriotic when voicing support, nevertheless, they rarely "kick-in and ante-up."

Through the years and until today, civil authorities have encountered a myriad of problems dealing with tax-exempt, profit-making religious entities that use the First Amendment's guarantee of freedom of religion to protect dubious activities. When a church or organization finds the need to have one or more lawyers on the payroll, one can almost be assured of unscrupulous and unethical dealings. More often than not, money—not just religion—is involved.

One prime example was L. Ronald Hubbard, a Nebraska-born science fiction writer who, in the 1950s, founded a network of mental health clinics that he later renamed the Church of Scientology. He lived a reclusive life in his opulent house.

Ron Hubbard was long a target of government fraud investigations in the U.S. and abroad. He lived out his final years in luxury at his ranch in the remote hills of central California, evading scores of lawsuits and surviving allegations by the Internal Revenue Service that he had secretly diverted more than one hundred million dollars of the Church of Scientology's assets to foreign bank accounts during the 1980's[19]."

Mr. Hubbard's successful evasion of federal investigation illustrated anew problems civil authorities encounter when in dealing with religious leaders suspected of exploiting the First Amendment's guarantee of freedom of religion to shield questionable activities. Churches and nonprofit organizations lack accountability. Many of these independent entities consider themselves above the law.

For example, in 1980, the state of California sought to place Pasadena-based Worldwide Church of God in receivership. Several of its members had contended that church leaders were stealing millions of dollars annually from member contributions. This outcry touched off numerous protests from leaders of other faiths. One official, Glen Holman, of the Ecumenical California Church Council said that "a state's right to examine a churches' financial record was in obvious violation of the First Amendment."[20] The state legislators of California soon passed a law repealing the right of any state law enforcement agencies to examine the books of religious groups except in very rare circumstances when criminal intent is expected. This legislation opened the door wider for the nation's largest church fundraising groups to resist government monitoring of their records.

"Mormonism"

As a very young lad I was introduced to the unethical fundraising tactics of the Church of Jesus Christ of Latter Day Saints—the Mormons. My mom and dad joined a local assembly when I was eleven years old.

This lasted for only about one year. However, during this brief period our family received numerous visits from the church elders.

In order to donate more money to the church, for example, it was suggested we cut back on groceries and family outings. My family's austerity measures would enable The Mormon Church in Utah to grow, expand, and be more influential, with the ultimate goal to put wealth at the top of the hierarchy and enhance the leadership's standard of living.

In the 1950's, The Mormon Church built an impregnable mountain vault some twenty miles southeast of Salt Lake City to provide earthquake-proof and bomb-proof security and stability for its genealogical microfilms, church records, and wealth. There are six openings in the sides of the mountain that lead into huge cross tunnels, which serve as storage areas. The interior is beautifully painted, lighted, and temperature and humidity controlled.

Mormonism has many strange doctrines and at its heart is racist and prejudiced. Evangelist Harry McGimsey in his folder, "Mormonism's Base Attack on Christianity," states:

The Mormon cult which condemns all Christian churches believes the following false doctrines: They believe that God is an exalted man, that Christ and the Devil are brothers, that Christ was married, that the Holy Spirit is a substance of fluid, and that there is salvation for the dead by proxy *(proxy 'of?'-check original)* water baptism, that there is no burning Hell; in genealogical research; plurality of wives; use of secret temples; in the fatherhood of God and the brotherhood of man; that people raise children after they leave the earth; in the pre-existence of man; that no Negro can hold the Mormon Priesthood or go through the secret Mormon temple."[21]

Mormonism is also prejudiced against other groups of people; however, the leadership will most definitely take their money.

"For the Love of Money"
For the love of money is the root of all evil;
which while some coveted after, they have erred from the faith.
—I Timothy 6:10

The newspaper articles that follow are examples of how evangelists have used non-biblical means to exploit the trust and "heart strings" of their parishioners to raise money.

"A Faith Healer's Death (Money) Wish"

Evangelist Oral Roberts told his flock Wednesday that God spared him because his followers contributed more than $8 million, but he also said he'll need that amount every year until the second coming of Christ.

It's April and I'm alive. And I'm on fire," the 69-year-old evangelist told a television audience Wednesday.

Roberts, who has drawn international attention since saying on Jan. 4 that God would "call him Home" if he didn't raise $8 million by the end of March, ended a ten-day vigil Tuesday night when he came down from his prayer tower at Oral Roberts University.

He also said his vigil had rejuvenated his healing power.

Roberts said the money would allow Oral Roberts University medical school students to graduate debt-free and become missionaries in Africa.

I don't want to misrepresent in any way, it takes time to turn it around. We must raise the $8 million every year, for the rest of our lives, until Jesus returns," Roberts said on his son's "Richard Roberts Live" television program. "It's a hard battle. And the Lord warned me when I came down from the prayer tower to tell you that we must continue doing this. There's no way out."

He said followers contributed $700,000 more than the original $8 million goal for scholarships. In addition, he said, financial problems that threatened his ministry's survival late last year had been remedied and the ministry's "support base" has a $400,000 surplus.

Richard Roberts announced Friday, after a Florida race track owner handed over a $1.3 million check March 23, that the $8 million goal for the scholarship program had been reached. But the elder Roberts indicated Tuesday that he still considered his life to be on the line.

Roberts said Wednesday the original goal first announced one year ago "was standing there like an adversary in our path."

Roberts has been criticized widely for saying God told him he would die unless the fund-raising goal was reached.

He said Tuesday the media and his critics had focused on the $8 million goal as "the more sensational."[22]

"Unorthodox Theft"

With a former church treasurer leveling charges of financial mismanagement, bishops of the Orthodox Church in America decided at a special meeting Wednesday to order audits and work toward tighter fiscal controls.

"To encourage financial accountability and trust," the ten bishops authorized a review of all special collections since 2001 and independent audits covering 2004 and 2005. They also vowed to implement such principles as "decisive financial governance" and "transparency of financial data."

Those steps, however, the check fell short of dissenters' demands for an audit of all church accounts over the past decade and a full-fledged investigation.

The bishops, who met at church headquarters in Syosset on Long Island, said they would continue work at their regular May meeting and possibly establish "a special committee of review."

The action came after allegations from the OCA's former treasurer, Protodeacon Eric Wheeler.

He says the church funds were spent on "embarrassing credit card debts," individuals who continually "leached off" family members and unspecified blackmail payments. Wheeler questioned accounting for millions of dollars in gifts and said no full, independent audit had occurred since 1996.

Last week, seventy one senior clergy urged the bishops to quickly launch an investigation of finances by a commission of bishops, priests and laity. Two weeks earlier, fifty-seven priests issued a similar petition.

Wheeler was an official at headquarters from 1988 until1999, the last three years as treasurer. He says he was dismissed after pressing for financial information. A church spokesman said no OCA officials were available to discuss the situation.

Wheeler sent his accusations last fall to the bishops and the Metropolitan Council, a governing body of thirty-one clergy and lay delegates–but neither body took action.[23]

"Regulators Warn on Religious Fraud"

Forrest Bomar, a retiree with most of his life savings in brokerage accounts, was tired of the market's swings and attracted by the 6.7-percent return offered on investments by the Baptist Foundation of Arizona.

He and his wife, Lee, are Baptists and were impressed by the salesman who came to their home in Tucson and seemed to share their values. "So we plunged in, repeatedly," Bomar recalled in an interview. "I was foolish enough to not ask for an annual report."

Now, the Bomars have lost nearly all of their $236,166 investment in what turned out to be a scam. The foundation declared bankruptcy and was shut down by state regulators, and three foundation officials have pleaded guilty to defrauding investors.

Forrest Bomar said he went through stages of disbelief, shock and deep depression from which he has not fully recovered. Still, in the end, he said Tuesday at a news conference, "My faith was tested; my faith was not taken." More than thirteen thousand people around the country, many of them elderly Baptists, invested some $590 million in the organization, state securities regulators said.

They are warning people to beware of proliferating and increasingly sophisticated investment schemes that play on religious loyalties. "I've seen more money stolen in the name of God than in any other way," Deborah Bortner, president of the North American Securities Administrators Association, said at the news conference with Bomar. The association represents securities regulators in the fifty states, the District of Columbia, Puerto Rico, Canada and Mexico.

"Always do your homework," urged Bortner, who also is Washington state's director of securities. "Be as skeptical and careful when you invest with someone who shares your faith as you would with anyone else." Promoters of investment schemes based on religion often predict an imminent financial or social crisis, or claim they will reinvest part of the profits in a worthy cause. Some perpetrators have kneeled to pray with their victims.

In the past three years, securities regulators in twenty-seven states have taken actions against hundreds of companies and individuals that used religious or spiritual beliefs to gain the trust of more than 90,000 investors. Bortner's warning came as the alleged mastermind behind the $448 million scheme of Greater Ministries International Church, based in Tampa, Fla., received a prison term. Gerald Payne, an ailing, sixty-five year-old minister, was sentenced Monday to twenty-seven years in prison on fraud charges.

The organization's promoters used Bible verses—like Luke 6:38: "Give, and it shall be given unto you"– promising the faithful that God would double their money if they gave it to Greater Ministries. Some twenty thousand investors nationwide were persuaded to mortgage their homes, run up big credit-card debts or cash in their retirement funds on the promise of huge returns from investments in cargo ships and gold, platinum, silver and diamond mines in the Caribbean and Africa, the regulators say.

Payne's wife, Betty, was sentenced to nearly thirteen years behind bars for her part in the scheme. Investigators have yet to find the missing millions, which they believe might be stashed in secret, offshore accounts. Gerald Payne waved feebly to supporters as he was led out of the courtroom in Tampa, where U.S. District Judge James Whittemore handed down the Paynes' sentences and chastised Gerald Payne as a "wolf in sheep's clothing."

"The fact that you used the word of God to perpetuate a fraud is absolutely despicable," Whittemore told Payne, who has suffered four strokes while in prison.

A third major case cited by the state regulators was that involving IRM Corp., which netted some $400 million from investors through the sale of bogus promissory notes and limited partnerships, said to be linked to the California real estate market. Before being shut down by Michigan regulators, the scheme had solicited investors through religious television and radio programs.

Regulators say the three cases—involving the Baptist Foundation of Arizona, Greater Ministries and IRM—all were Ponzi schemes, in which new investors are continually recruited to make payments to previous investors until it all collapses.[24]

While there are numerous 'scam artists' getting caught, the percentage is much too small. Many pastors, evangelists, and charismatic leaders are robbing individuals with words and psychology. My goal is to enlighten the public, especially poor and elderly, to be knowledgeable and vigilant about the goals of all religious and nonprofit organizations.

> *Beware of the false prophets, who come to you in sheep's clothing, but inwardly are ravenous wolves.*
> —Matthew 7:15

"Nonprofit Groups Funneled Money for Abramoff"

Politics and the Religious Right

Funds Flowed to Lobbying Campaigns

Newly released documents in the Jack Abramoff investigation shed light on how the lobbyist secretly routed his clients' funds through tax-exempt organizations with the acquiescence of those in charge, including prominent conservative activist Grover Norquist.

The federal probe has brought a string of bribery-related charges and plea deals. The possible misuse of tax-exempt groups is also receiving investigators' attention, sources familiar with the matter said.

Among the organizations used by Abramoff was Norquist's Americans for Tax Reform. According to an investigative report on Abramoff's lobbying released last week by the Senate Indian Affairs

Committee, Americans for Tax Reform served as a "conduit" for funds that flowed from Abramoff's clients to surreptitiously finance grass-roots lobbying campaigns. As the money passed through, Norquist's organization kept a small cut, e-mails show.

A second group Norquist was involved with the Council of Republicans for Environmental Advocacy received about $500,000 in Abramoff client funds; the council's president has told Senate investigators that Abramoff often asked her to lobby a senior Interior Department official on his behalf. The committee report said the Justice Department should further investigate the organization's dealings with the department and its former deputy secretary, J. Steven Griles.

Norquist has long been an architect of tax-cutting policies and political strategies that have boosted the Republican Party. He and Abramoff have been close since their days as young conservative leaders of the College Republicans more than two decades ago.

The Senate committee report also details Abramoff's dealings with two others from the College Republicans crowd: Ralph Reed, former Christian Coalition executive director; and Amy Moritz Ridenour, president of the National Center for Public Policy Research, which sponsored a golf trip in 2000 to Scotland for then-Rep. Tom DeLay (R-Tex). Ralph Reed's companies received a total of more than $5 million to run Abramoff lobbying effort.

"Call Ralph re Grover doing pass through," Abramoff wrote in a stark e-mail reminder to himself in 1999, a year in which Norquist moved more than $1 million in Abramoff client money to Reed and Christian anti-gambling groups. Reed was working to defeat lotteries and casinos that would have competed with Abramoff's tribal and Internet gambling clients.

In a recent interview at The Washington Post, Norquist said that Americans for Tax Reform and Abramoff's gambling clients worked together because they shared anti-tax, anti-regulatory views. He denied that Americans for Tax Reform was used to conceal the source of funds sent to Reed. Reed reiterated in a statement last week that he did not know the money he received originated as the proceeds of gambling at Indian casinos.

All told in 1999, the Choctaws gave Americans for Tax Reform $1.15 million, most of which ATR passed on to Reed's for-profit political consulting company, Century Strategies, and Christian anti-gambling groups working to defeat a state lottery in Alabama.

Norquist said in The Post interview that the Choctaw tribe originally wanted ATR to direct the anti-lottery campaign, but his organization decided that it would be better to assist Christian groups already fighting the lottery.

"When we looked at it, we said they have an actual ongoing effort, we don't need to run it and [could instead] just contribute there, which was a continuation of the previous coalition," Norquist said. "They said fine."

But Choctaw representative Nell Rogers told Senate Indian Affairs Committee investigators that ATR "was not involved and was not considering getting involved in any efforts the Choctaw ultimately paid Reed and others to oppose," the committee reported." Rogers told the committee staff that she understood from Abramoff that ATR was willing to serve as a conduit, provided it received a fee," the report said. Rogers said the tribe had a long relationship with Americans for Tax Reform and assumed that the fee "would simply be used to support the overall activity of ATR."

Abramoff, however, grew annoyed at the amount that Norquist took off the top before sending the money on, e-mails show. "Grover kept another $25 k!" Abramoff wrote in a February 2000 note to himself.

John Kartch, a spokesman for Americans for Tax Reform, said Friday that the group was not involved in Abramoff's lobbying business. The Choctaw tribe, he said, "was a longtime supporter of ATR. They had no business dealings with Grover Norquist, nor did Jack Abramoff."

E-mails show that Abramoff also moved client money through a conservative Jewish foundation called Toward Tradition, run by longtime Abramoff friend Rabbi Daniel Lapin. In January 2000, when Reed sent Abramoff an $867,000 invoice to be billed to a Choctaw official, Abramoff responded: "Ok, thanks. Please get me the groups we are using, since I want to give this to her all at once." Reed responded: "Amy, Grover, Lapin and one other I will get you."

Abramoff tapped the same cluster of tax-exempt groups in 2000 to help defeat legislation to ban gambling on the Internet. Abramoff's client, an online gambling services company called eLottery, donated money to ATR, the policy research center and Toward Tradition.

In May 2000, just before a key vote on the anti-gambling bill, the research center paid for the Scotland trip for then-House Majority Whip DeLay. Toward Tradition hired the wife of DeLay aide Tony C. Rudy, who later pleaded guilty to conspiring to corrupt public officials, saying his wife was paid in exchange for his official actions. Lapin has said his hiring of Lisa Rudy was not connected to any eLottery donations.

Americans for Tax Reform received $160,000 from eLottery, and Norquist immediately sent most of the money to a state nonprofit group, which in turn sent the money to another Ralph Reed company to fund attack ads on Republicans who supported the gambling ban. In the interview, Norquist denied that the purpose of the transfer was to hide the money's origin.

"Someone from eLottery talked to me or somebody on our staff and said, 'Will you help us with this campaign?' and we said, 'We're certainly supportive of it,' and they gave us resources and asked if we would contribute to the state group," Norquist said.

Norquist said he could not remember if he knew at the time that eLottery was an Abramoff client, but he said it would not have made any difference.[25]

CHAPTER 6

ELECTRIC CHURCH

"The scriptural means of supporting the works of the gospel is through free will offerings of God's people. All other ways are unscriptural and usually carnal."
—Radio Bible Class

In the United States, where we have a high degree of individualism and diverse cultural societies, there is a strong tendency to exalt leaders and elevate personalities. Television evangelists are no different and their audience is often deceived into thinking that what they say 'in the name' of Jesus is truth. These charlatans focus on evoking feelings and not what the Bible says. Feelings are subjective and relative, whereas, truth is made to understand, meditate on, and live as best we can. Our generation is biblically unsound and has a tendency to rely on feelings, emotions and false manifestations. The modern televangelist knows and exploits the ignorance of society and tells them what they want to hear; not the truths they need to hear.

The fundamental premise of the "Electric Church" is the beaming of messages and preaching services over the airways by means of television. The modern televangelist knows that TV is King of the advertising media and they use it to their advantage. Annually the electric church is a billion dollar business. The best televangelists are 50% salesman, 40% performer and 10% preacher. There was no person any better at televangelism than the fallen Jimmy Swaggart. He was a pioneer in achieving wealth and fame by captivating and entertaining his audiences. A journalist proclaiming Jimmy Swaggart's prowess from the pulpit once said the following:

"Mr. Swaggart has called himself 'an old-fashioned, Holy Ghost-filled, shouting, weeping, soul-winning, gospel-preaching preacher.' But that description does not come close to capturing his power. He turns each service into an epic exploration of sin and redemption, roaring the gospel in a rough bayou bark and singing it in a smoky baritone. Mr. Swaggart has been perhaps the most visible symbol of the enormous growth in Pentecostalism. The movement has been the fastest growing segment of religion in America for the last decade because of its ecstatic, theatrical tenor and emphasis on powerful personal experience through 'gifts of the Spirit' like faith healing and speaking in tongues."[26]

Jimmy Swaggart is considered more of a performer than a preacher. His piano playing and singing expertise, preaching with his backwoods apocalyptic preaching style, was the quintessential hero of some thirty million members of the various Spirit-filled Christian faiths. As far back as the late 1980's, before Swaggart's extra-marital affairs with women in wayside motels were exposed, his electronic empire was amassing nearly $150 million annually.

I can remember seeing Jimmy Swaggart's wife and son on television, after being exposed of his profligious living, crying on behalf of their husband and father. This was in reality an appeal to the audience not to stop sending in donations. The Swaggart family owns a tremendous amount of property and real estate in the Baton Rouge, Louisiana area.

Televangelism has two unique mitigations: first, it allots fundamental Bible preaching equal time against secular humanists; and secondly, it gives people like "shut-ins" the opportunity for a church service. The big question is how are they exploiting these "shut-ins?" Chicanery and deceitfulness are often used in raising contributions to support the ministries.

Mel White, better known as the "ghost writer" of the 1980's was employed by Pat Robertson, Jerry Falwell, and others to write fundraising letters for television audiences. Mel, a professional, is also a homosexual minister and currently operates a church for gays and lesbians in Texas. The lifestyle that Mel White engages in was vocally condemned by Falwell and Robertson to be an "abomination unto God." However, while he was an employee, his lifestyle was overlooked because of his great talent and the money brought into the ministries as a direct result of his writings.

Another means by which the public is cheated involves the exploitation of television stars or professional athletes—people who will sell you a Bible on Sunday morning and a bottle of booze on Sunday afternoon. Now, a can of one's favorite "gusto" will not send you to eternal damnation, however, athletes should be prudent when advertising their image before teenagers and children.

Fundraising tactics had gotten so immoral that the Reverend Billy Graham said: "Evangelicals and religious broadcasters do not need gimmicks and high-pressure professional fund-raising tactics to accomplish God's work. We must have the highest standards in morality, ethics, and integrity if we are to continue to have influence." The church has become a theater with a stage, players, an audience, and preachers making clowns of themselves. Our clergy is befitting "professional beggars" utilizing prose and gimmicks rather than faith and character.

> *"But without faith it is impossible to please him: for he that cometh to God must believe that he is, and that he is a rewarder of them that diligently seek him."*
> —Hebrews 11:6

Electric Church

The following is a true story, one that is common to televangelism. In 1988, an elderly Oregon widow felt moved to become a Faith Partner of the Old-Time Gospel Hour, having become a devotee of Jerry Falwell and several other television evangelists while nursing her dying husband. After making her pledge to send ten dollars per month, she received the following certified letter from Falwell:

At this moment, I am being forced to make some decisions that are literally breaking my heart–it is two A.M. and I am sitting at the kitchen table. And as one of my loyal Faith Partners I knew you'd want to know immediately.

I've just received the annual year-end analysis of the Old-Time Gospel Hour television and radio stations. And I'm sorely disappointed to find that many of our stations are NOT self-supporting financially.

Since we have no other means of underwriting a station except through the support of loyal friends like you and local people who receive the station, it may be necessary to remove The Old-Time Gospel Hour from a large number of stations.

This truly grieves my spirit. I also believe this grieves the Lord. And unless we can turn this situation around, I will have to stop broadcasting God's Word over these stations very soon—I may even have to cut the station over which you receive The Old-Time Gospel Hour in your home.

This is why I'm going to ask if you could possibly consider making a sacrificial gift to The Old-Time Gospel Hour, and if possible send your full payment of $120 for 1988 today.

This was followed by a second letter within a week and on the back of the letters from Falwell to her, the widow made her reply, as follows:

Dear Pastor Jerry,

I am so sorry you are so hard up for money for many things, especially for television time; yes, I will truly miss your Sunday morning service.

My dear husband has departed this life and gone home to be with his Lord and I surely miss him; but, I have been able to start back to my local church and it's not so hard on me as it would have been six months ago when I was so tied down taking care of my dear husband. Your service and Rex Humbard and Oral Roberts all were such a blessing to me and then I listened to my local church at 11 o'clock on the radio.

Pastor, I'll send you my whole Faith Partners promise for this year now, but I won't be able to continue to send each month. I am a senior citizen and I have only so much coming in. I am looking forward to getting my special giant print Bible; I have been working with an unsaved friend so I am giving her one of my Bibles I already have.

Thank you for your nice letter and thank you for the Christian lady who wrote to me.

I am still on heavy sleeping medicine, also nerve pills and they're for medicine to help me remember things. I completely forget things I should remember, etc. I have to write it all down; but I am doing better and I do feel the Lord will raise me up. Thank you for your prayers.

The letters from Falwell were written automatically by a computer program used by The Old Time Gospel Hour for fundraising.

> *"Beware of the scribes, which desire to walk in long robes, and love greetings in the markets, and the highest seats in the synagogues, and the chief rooms at feast; which DEVOUR widows houses, and for a show make long prayers; the same shall receive greater damnation."*
> —Luke 20:46, 47

Preface to "TBN"

Besides living a lavish lifestyle, extremely high salaries, and numerous vacationing homes, where else might your donations be going? *The Los Angeles Times* reported that "Paul Crouch, the President of Trinity Broadcasting Network (TBN) paid Enoch Lonnie Ford $425,000 in 1998 in settlement over what Ford argued was an unjust dismissal from working at TBN. The settlement contained several other points, among them an agreement for Lonnie Ford to keep silent about an alleged homosexual encounter they had in 1996 at a TBN-owned cabin near Lake Arrowhead, California."[27] In a statement released on September 22, 2004, TBN denied Paul Crouch had a homosexual affair with Ford, but did confirm the payment of $425,000 to Mr. Ford.

One thing Paul Crouch has on his side is some powerful friends. Paul was brought up in the same Missouri town as John Ashcroft, President George Bush's former fundamentalist attorney general. Paul Crouch and TBN supported Ashcroft during his Senate confirmation process in January 2001. Hour upon hour for support was supplied in programming with your donated money. Did Crouch ask the country's top law officer for return favors?

The Crouches are very vehement against anyone who criticizes them or TBN. In 1997, Crouch made the following threat, "God, we proclaim death to anything or anyone that will lift a hand against this network and this ministry that belongs to you, God."[28]

A few years earlier, he reacted even more fervently to critics he characterized as "heresy hunters."

"To hell with you!" he raved during a praise-a-thon in 1991. "Quit blocking God's bridges or God's going to shoot you—if I don't."[29]

I know that in the past Paul Crouch and Benny Hinn have made statements about "calling on the demons of HELL" to attack any and all individuals who criticize TBN. I believe, however, if Crouch and his band of performers would have their spiritual temperatures measured in gunpowder, it would not be enough to blow their noses. TBN contains very little that is Godly; only a mixture of hype, worldly entertainment, and the rowdiness of a Texas barroom. The vast majority of the performers have bulging wallets to match that challenges the growth rate of the Chinese economy. They really need a great deal more temperance and not your money.

"He who lives without discipline dies without honor."
—Icelandic Proverb

"TBN (Trinity Broadcast Network)"

Trinity Broadcasting Network, or TBN, is the world's largest Chrisitan television network, founded by Paul and Jan Crouch in 1973, the network now has a larger U.S. viewership than its three main competitor networks combined. It owns twenty-three U.S. full-power television stations and 252 low-power rural stations, and has a viewership in excess of five million U.S. households per week. The network has grown to forty-seven satellites and 12,500 affiliates, reaching almost 100,000,000 households globally. Today Paul Crouch is the network's president and chairman and wife, Jan Crouch is its vice president and program director. Paul Jr. is the vice president for administration, and the network maintains production deals with their other son, Matthew.

The network has attracted attention for its continuous fundraising activities, including the "prosperity gospel," an offshoot of the Word of Faith doctrine that appears to promise donors, including those who barely have enough money for their own living expenses, that God will make them rich as long as they have faith and give to TBN.[30] Paul Crouch has continuously made "inciteful" statements along the lines of, "Have you got something that you have been praying about ten, fifteen, twenty years? You have been praying for it and haven't gotten it?" Then, providing a response to his own question, "people haven't received it because they haven't given their ten percent." During a 1997 program, he said, cavalierly that if "you have been healed or saved or blessed through TBN and have not contributed you are robbing God and will lose your reward in heaven."[31]

> The Trinity Broadcast enterprise profits more than $100 million annually. They got an offer to sell in 1998 but the Crouches refused the offer—it was valued at nearly $2 billion at the time. In 2004, Paul Crouch's salary was reported at $403,700 and Jan's at $361,000.[32]

Televangelists like the Crouches have a very visible profile that reflects a view of 'pastorship' throughout today's church community. Now the "local churches" compares preachers in their pulpits to them, thinking they too are out to gain wealth. Many have become leery of the church for this reason. They sit back and observe what is unfolding before them on TBN and other networks like it and are either taken in by it, or turned off so much so that they become mistrustful of their own church leadership.

The following article is reprinted in part with permission of *Cutting Edge*.

"TBN: Temple of the Greek God and Goddess"
Subtitled:
When you understand the unchristian doctrines being promoted by TBN, your skin will crawl with horror! You will realize that TBN is "Christian in Appearance Without Being Christian in Theology"—When you hear Kenneth Copeland call God a Failure, you will know the truth.

Remember the warning from the apostle Paul?

"Let no one deceive or beguile you in any way, for that day will not come except the apostasy comes first—unless the predicted great falling away of those who have professed to be Christians has come—and the man of lawlessness (sin) is revealed, who is the son of doom (of perdition)."
—2 Thessalonians 2:3

Such false Christian churches are prophesied as opening the door to the Antichrist. The New World Order is coming. Are you ready? Once you understand what this New World Order really is, and how it is being gradually implemented, you will be able to see it progressing in your daily news. Learn how to protect yourself, your loved ones. Stand by for insights so startling you will never look at the news the same way again.

You are Now on the Cutting Edge.

Paw Creek Ministries Note: "The majority of the information contained in this article was taken from Trinity Broadcast Network telecasts. I personally listened to every word from the voices of each person quoted in this article."

If there is one thing certain about Paul and Jan Crouch, it is that nothing is certain. Whether the guest of Trinity Broadcast Network is a religious leader who is fairly fundamental in doctrine or a "way-out" person who says almost nothing that makes Biblical sense, they both are welcomed and applauded as great teachers. For one hour of the "Praise

The Lord" show, you may hear someone trusted by much of the church world, preaching the Truth, but the next hour hear the babble of Kim Clement. Theology, or Biblical truth, is just not important to TBN.

TBN Is Religious Entertainment

In fact, Paul Crouch calls Biblical theology "doo-doo". On a *Praise The Lord* telecast, he shouted, "Let Him (God) sort out all this doctrinal doo-doo, I don't care about it". He apparently hates no one worse than those he calls "heresy hunters". On another occasion he spoke to his worldwide audience by stating, "Heretic hunters, those guys who spend their lives straightening us all out doctrinally, they are going to go straight to hell." (You could hear Jan laughing approvingly on the set.)

Here are a man and woman that control the message about the Word of God and the airing of the messages of the most noted televangelists to the greatest single audience in the world, yet they hate correction and Biblical reproof. Listen to God's warning:

> *"Correction is grievous unto him that forsaketh the way: and he that hateth reproof shall die."* [Prov 15:10]

This is a formula for spiritual disaster and that is what is already occurring. When Crouch, Hinn, and Copeland are displaying such a hatred for anyone who will dare Biblically reprove them, God's correction, when it comes, will be both "grievous" and "deadly."

Now listen to three additional statements that show Paul Crouch's disdain for anyone that dares to question the messages of his guests on Trinity Broadcast Network

Transcribed From Trinity Broadcasting Network "Praise The Lord" Show:

- "I refuse to argue any longer with any of you out there. Don't even call me if you want to argue doctrine, If you want to straighten somebody out over here, if you want to criticize Kenneth Copeland for his preaching on faith of Dad Hagin, get out of my life. I don't ever want to talk to you or hear, I don't want to see your ugly face."

- "I think they are damned and on their way to hell and I don't think there is any redemption for them. I say, 'to hell with you'."

- "I say, 'Get out of God's way, quit blocking God's bridges (Apparently, he defines God's bridges as the One World Church and Ecumenism of the coming Kingdom of Antichrist).

- "God is going to shoot you if I don't"

What Do Paul And Jan Really Believe?

Either they do not know what they believe or they do not care. Their guests present some of the wildest possible heresies that can possibly be spread to a gullible audience. Two of their newest stars/idols are Phil Munsey and Kim Clement. The mainstays of the last five to twenty years have come from well-known Tel-evangelists that continually teach questionable doctrines that have already destroyed a multitude of believers. We want to simply provide quotes from TBN telecasts and their guests and then compare those quotes to the light of clear biblical truth. The picture that will emerge will represent some of the absolute darkest heresies available in the christian church world. The problem is that these TBN people—whose actual words you will read—are not called cultic, or unchristian. They operate in the supposedly sane world of true Christianity. You must let God's Word help you recognize the truth. Your spiritual life and your eternal destiny are absolutely at stake.

The "Force of Faith" vs. The "Faith of our Fathers"

Nothing we discuss in this article is more important than this definition of faith—saving faith. God is either the Sovereign and Eternal

God that has revealed Himself in His book of faith (The Holy Bible) or He is a pagan god that operates much like Kenneth Hagin, Kenneth Copeland, Benny Hinn, Paul Crouch, and others describe. Listen carefully to this explanation of TBN faith.

- Kenneth Copeland: "The force of faith is in the spiritual realm a great deal like certain forces in the natural realm. It is a spiritual force, like gravity is a natural force, and electricity is a natural force of power."

- Paul Crouch: "A measurable natural force."

- Kenneth Copeland: "It's a measurable force, it's conductible, it's perceptible to the touch...Faith is a spiritual tone, it's perceptible,... It is a tangible force, it's an invisible force, so is gravity, but it is there."

- Paul Crouch: "So is electricity.. Does God use faith?"

- Kenneth Copeland: "Surely."

- Paul Crouch: "...See, here is the sore spot. There are those who say..."

- Jan Crouch: "Not with him." (speaking of Copeland)

- Paul Crouch: "Not with you." (lots of laughter follows)

- Jan Crouch: "Not with God."

- Kenneth Copeland "..the fact. No, I'm not sore at God at all and I don't think He's sore at me...I haven't done anything to Him."

- Paul Crouch: "... The critics say God is God, He doesn't have to have faith; He doesn't exercise faith. He doesn't use faith. He's God. He's the object of faith."

- Kenneth Copeland: "...Wait a minute, what does that mean? Object of faith. I don't know what that means."

- Jan Crouch: "I don't either."

Can you believe the Biblical ignorance on display with the "Reverend" Ken Copeland and Jan Crouch, as they admit they do not understand what "Object of faith" means? It means the Person to Whom we direct our faith! God is that Object, because He alone is Worthy, Omnipotent, Eternal, and Omniscient. We direct our "saving faith" to Jesus Christ alone, for He alone is worthy and He alone is the One to Whom God the Father has entrusted all matters of judgment and reward [John 5:22]

What Does The Bible Say About Faith?

The definition of Biblical faith has no kinship to this "Force of Faith" espoused by Copeland, and Paul and Jan Crouch. In the above statement by Kenneth Copeland, God is said to use faith just like Copeland uses faith. Faith ceases to be the lofty and eternal truth forever settled in the Heavens and established by an eternal God that is Himself the Object of our faith. But, to TBN, this faith becomes a formula or a New Age force that is a pagan idea, clearly akin to the many teachings of the occult.

In fact, Copeland's teaching is straight from the Antichrist! Listen:

The new religion of the Antichrist is prophesied to be a religion of "forces". Daniel prophesied this clear warning.

'But in his estate shall he honor the God of forces: and a god whom his fathers knew not shall he honor with gold, and silver, and with precious stones, and pleasant things.' [Daniel 11:38]

To even suggest faith as a "force" is to deny God as an eternal being to whom we turn in truth and faith for all our sufficiency, and for our solid hope of eternal life in Heaven. It actually reduces God to the level of man. Real faith is clearly seen in Apostle Paul's beautiful description to the Hebrews. Listen to his biblical statement of faith:

"Now faith is the substance of things hoped for, the evidence of things not seen."

"Through faith we understand that the worlds were framed by the word of God, so that things which are seen were not made of things which do appear."

"But without faith it is impossible to please Him: for he that cometh to God must believe that he is, and that he is a rewarder of them that diligently seek him."
[Hebrews 11:1,3,6].

In true Faith God is the "Absolute, the Eternal Sovereign God" in whom we rest all our hopes.

This is our greatest assurance! Doctrines are the anchor of our soul, especially as we face eternity! To deny key doctrines is to take away our greatest single source of assurance and spiritual confidence! Why would any leader want to take away precious spiritual confidence in our eternal destiny by repudiating key doctrines of the Faith?

Copeland: God is the Biggest "Failure" in the Bible

When you join together the concept of faith as a "force" with a God that became the biggest failure in the universe, you are laying the foundation for a "pagan cult" or a "paranormal religion".

Listen to this TBN telecast where biblical doctrines are cast to the wind:

- Kenneth Copeland: "I was shocked when I found out who the biggest failure in the Bible actually is."

- Paul Crouch: "Okay."

- Kenneth Copeland: "You know everybody you ask, you say, 'Who's the biggest failure?' They say, 'Judas' Somebody else will say, 'No! I believe it was Adam.' Well, how about the devil?"

- Paul Crouch: (Sound of amazement)
- Kenneth Copeland: "He's the most consistent failure..., but he's not the biggest in terms of material failure and so forth. The biggest in the whole Bible is God.... Wait, wait. Don't you turn that set off. You listen to us. I told you.... Now, you sit still a minute. You know me well enough to know I wouldn't tell something I can't prove by the Bible.

- "He lost His top ranking of His most anointed angel, the first man He ever created, the first woman He ever created, the whole earth and all the fullness therein, a third of the angels at least. That's a big loss, man! I mean, you figure up all of that, that's a lot of real estate, gone down the drain. Now, the reason you don't think of God as a failure, He never said He's a failure. (Paul Crouch and others laughing on the set.) And you are not a failure until you say you are one."

This definition of "failure" is ridiculous. A person is a failure if they do not reach a certain standard set beforehand. This definition of "failure" is at least as ridiculous as the statement said to me one day by a salesman trying to convince me it was just fine to lie to my clients.

"David, it is not a lie if, when you say it, you are smiling." You laugh at this nonsense, but Copeland's definition of a "failure" is just as ridiculous.

Does The Bible Suggest That God Was A Failure?

Our Sovereign God created us in His image that we might bring honor and glory to Him and have eternal fellowship together. He desired our love and He wanted that love to be our choice. He wanted our obedience, but He wanted that obedience to be *our choice*. To suggest that God was a failure because Adam and Eve made a sinful choice is ridiculous; such error is the kind of disinformation you would expect from the chief enemy of God, Satan himself! Such belief completely alters the entire Biblical account of man's fall, Satan's fall, and the terrible results that occurred. Our world would certainly be a different place if man had not sinned, but not for one moment was God ever a failure. The only failure was found in those that sinned. He never ceased to be the God of His universe or of the spiritual world where His Will is forever being done.

If you believe God was, and is, a failure, you reduce Him to mere man. Therefore, you have instantly obliterated all—I repeat, ALL—of the great and precious promises of the Bible! Every single promise relating to Redemption, Justification, Eternal Salvation, "No Condemnation" [John 3:18; Romans 8:1], and so many other promises are instantly obliterated! This belief renders the Bible worthless and invalid. Your study of the Bible and commentaries and good study materials on individual books of the Bible and important topics are now exercises in futility if you believe this nonsense. You gravitate toward "Christian psychology", which is exactly where the Christian Bookstore Industry is languishing right now.

The Biblical account of the years that have transpired since Satan's fall are filled with God's story and the revelations that have never ceased to unfold. King David made it clear who rules this Universe and it has never been the devil. His inspired words speak volumes.

"The earth is the LORD'S, and the fulness thereof; the world, and they that dwell therein. For he hath founded it upon the seas, and established it upon the floods. Who shall ascend into the hill of the LORD? or who shall stand in his holy place? He that hath clean hands, and a pure heart; who hath not lifted up his soul unto vanity, nor sworn deceitfully. He shall receive the blessing from the LORD, and righteousness from the God of his salvation. This is the generation of them that seek him, that seek thy face, O Jacob. Selah. Lift up your heads, O ye gates; even lift them up, ye everlasting doors; and the King of glory shall come in. Who is this King of glory? The LORD strong and mighty, the LORD mighty in battle. Lift up your heads, O ye gates; even lift them up, ye everlasting doom; and the King of glory shall come in. Who is this King of glory? The LORD of hosts, he is the King of glory. Selah." [Psalm 24:1-10]

You have the choice of believing Copeland, the Crouches, TBN, and the Charismatic Movement, or God and His true prophets. Reducing God is a constant theme of these diluted pundits (self-proclaimed authorities), but His majesty is undefeatable.

The foolishness of this crowd gets worse.

The Deity Of The Son Of God In Question

Always, spiritual error is on a downward spiral. Truth ascends and gets richer and sweeter, but error descends and becomes more and more absurd, and more and more bitter. That is clearly the direction of Paul and Jan Crouch. We will see other evidence of that direction in some of the new stars of TBN, but already, the deity of Jesus Christ is under attack. Read carefully the following conversation:

- Kenneth Copeland: "We are still questioning what was said about that prophecy. That prophecy never mentioned the Son of God. Never said anything about the Son of God."

- Paul Crouch: "What did it say?"

- Kenneth Copeland: ' "It said, 'I did not claim to be God'."

- Jan Crouch: (Unintelligible sounds.)

- Kenneth Copeland: "That's all it said."

- Paul Crouch: "In other words, in so many words, you're right, no where in the New Testament did he literally get up…"

- Kenneth Copeland: "…preach and claim that He was God…"

- Paul Crouch: "…and say, 'I am, God.' Did He? I stand corrected."

Here is the apparent "new word of prophecy" that was being discussed by Copeland and Crouch. It is an example of the "new revelations" as being claimed throughout the 'New Wave' so-called revival. Jesus Christ supposedly told Copeland the following "new revelation":

"Don't be disturbed when people put you down and speak harshly and roughly of you. They spoke that way of Me, should they not speak that way of you? The more you get to be like Me, the more they're going to think that way of you. They crucified Me for claiming that I was God. But I didn't claim I was God; I just claimed I walked with Him and He was in Me. Hallelujah." (Kenneth Copeland, "Take Time To Pray." *Believer's Voice of Victory*, 15:2, February 1987:9).

Did you catch that pertinent phrase from Copeland's "new revelation" from Jesus? Let us read that quote again, as "Jesus" is speaking:

"They crucified Me for claiming that I was God. But I didn't claim I was God; I just claimed I walked with Him and He was in Me." [Emphasis added]

Let us quickly review the many Biblical instances in which Jesus claimed to be God. Notice all these verses are Jesus' Words:

- Jesus calls Himself "I AM" (God's name as He told Moses—Exodus 3:14)—John 8:58—*"Before Abraham was, I AM"*—This declaration from Jesus' lips is the absolute strongest declaration Jesus made about being God. Only God is the great "I AM".

- Was Creator God—John 1:1-3, 15

- Was Equal With The Father—Matthew 11:27; Proverbs 30:49

- Jesus Is Eternal As Is the Father—John 1:1-4, 15; 6:62; 8:23, 58; 17:5, 24-25;

- Will Be Exalted In Heaven Equal With The Father—Like 22:69; 24:26; John 13:31;

- Holiness Equal To God—Mark 1:24; 4:34, admission by demons; Luke 1:35; John 16:10

- Claims to Be King of Glory—Matthew 21:5, 31-34; 26:64; 27:11; 28:18; Luke 1:32; 19:27; 22:29-30; John 12:15; 18:37

- Claims To Be The Divine Messiah—Matthew 26:63-64; Mark 12:35-37; Luke 24:25-27; John 8:14-18

- Claimed Power To Forgive Sins—Matthew 9:2-6; Mark 2:5-10; Luke 5:20-24; 7:47-50

I could literally fill pages with references demonstrating that Jesus most certainly did make many claims to be God, doing so repeatedly. These Words of Jesus Himself demonstrate the complete and utter bankruptcy of Copeland's "new revelation" and completely proves the unbiblical and spiritually dangerous realm called "New Revelation" or "Prophetic Utterances", or "Word of Prophecy". If you ever followed this nonsense before, you now know the truth, and that truth shall surely set you free!

Here is an additional quote by Copeland, which confirms his belief that Jesus was not God as He appeared on earth. "What (why) does God have to pay the price for this thing? He has to have a man that is like that first one. It's got to be a man. He's got to be all man. He cannot be a God and come storming in here with attributes and dignities that are not common to man. He can't do that. It's not legal." (Kenneth Copeland, "Question &Answer", *Believer's Voice of Victory* 16. 8 (August 1, 1988):8, emphasis in original.)

In other words, Kenneth Copeland separates the 100% Divine Jesus from the 100% Human. He is saying Jesus is only human, but not also God.

This is the Biblical definition of Antichrist!! Listen:

"And every spirit which does not acknowledge and confess that Jesus Christ has come in the flesh, but would...sever, disunite Him, is not of God, does not proceed from Him. This nonconfession is the spirit of the antichrist, of

which you heard that it was coming, and now it is already in the world." [1 John 4:3]

Thus, when Kenneth Copeland states that Jesus cannot be all man plus all God, he is speaking from the spirit of Antichrist! Doubt it not! When you watch the video, *"Kenneth Hagen: Spirit of the Serpent"*, you will see Copeland dancing and jerking and rolling his eyes like you would expect from a man possessed.

Let's read the words of another guest that was also bold enough to deny the deity of the Lord Jesus Christ.

Transcribed From Trinity Broadcasting Network's "Praise The Lord Show":

Joseph Good: "Yeshua (Jesus), we do not see as being God when He walked here on earth. We see Him as a man."
Guest: "A man anointed by God."
Joseph Good: "A man anointed by God, sent by God to perform a function. Now, in his resurrection…"
Guest: "He's not God."
Joseph Good: "We do not see Him as God. We see Him as a man anointed by God. And that has been restored. There is nothing in the statements of Yeshua, in the statements of the disciples, that would cause one to believe that they were proclaiming that He was deity."

In addition to denying that Jesus ever claimed to be God—Deity—this speaker goes more boldly than Copeland into declaring that Jesus was a mere man upon Whom the "Christ Consciousness" spirit fell. Once this spirit fell upon Him, Jesus then became the World Teacher, the Messiah. But, He never was God. This teaching is straight out of the New Age Pit of the Abyss! New Agers believe that the same Christ Conscious Spirit that fell upon Jesus in His time also fell on Buddha in his time and Mohammed in his time, and will also fall upon the coming World Teacher who will call himself Maitreya—the Biblical Antichrist! Thus, can you see that the teachings of this TBN crowd is purely Antichrist! Doubt it not!! Their own words condemn them.

Copeland: Jesus Became Divine Son Only After He Had Been "Born Again In Hell"

The Copeland, Hagin, Hinn, and Crouch, theology plainly teaches that Jesus was only human in His earthly visit. Paul Crouch makes a statement that Jesus was reincarnated as the Divine Son when He was "born again" in hell. Let's listen to Kenneth Copeland say that God was not the Father of Jesus Christ, that He was an *"emaciated (poured out) little wormy spirit..., down in the bottom of that thing (the pit of hell)."* Then, we hear Benny Hinn say how Jesus was again with Paul Crouch, adding, "that is when his divinity returned?'

Did you catch that totally blasphemous statement from "Reverend" Kenneth Copeland? He described the glorious Jesus Christ, Eternal God, Creator of the Universe, and Final Judge, in a most disgusting way. Listen again:

Jesus was an *"emaciated (poured out) little wormy spirit.., down in the bottom of that thing (the pit of hell)."*

If you are a follower of this crowd, you can hear Jesus warn: *'Wherefore by their fruits ye shall know them."* [Matt 7:16-20]

Copeland Declares Jesus Took on Nature of Satan!

Copeland: "How did Jesus then on the cross say, 'My God!' Because God was not His Father any more. He took upon Himself the nature of Satan. And I'm telling you Jesus is in the middle of that pit. He's suffering all that there is to suffer, there is no suffering left.. . apart from Him. His emaciated, little wormy spirit is down in the bottom of that thing and the devil thinks He's got Him destroyed. But, all of a sudden God started talking."

Now, Copeland has the gall to actually say that Jesus took the nature of Satan! The only reason Jesus could be the Savior of you and me, taking our sins upon Him, was because He was Perfect! God the Father could only accept the sacrificial gift from a Perfect Savior! If Jesus could be soiled in any manner, He would no longer be Perfect and His sacrifice on the Cross would be for nothing. The Bible teaches that Jesus was Perfect to the very end, to the moment He "gave up the ghost" and died in His physical body. Study these Scriptures to see for yourself that Jesus was absolutely perfect!

Benny Hinn then gets into the act of speaking astonishing things against the Lord of Lords and King of Kings, attempting to deny the complete Perfection of Jesus.

> Benny Hinn: "Jesus Christ destroyed the power of Satan on earth, but destroyed Satan in the underworld, the Holy Ghost wasn't there. Think about that."
> Paul Crouch: "That's when His divinity returned."

To suggest that there was ever a time when Jesus was not Divine is Antichrist heresy, but it fully fits in with Copeland's remarks, above. Now that both Copeland and Hinn have soiled the absolute "Perfections" of Jesus Christ, let us briefly study what the Bible has to say:

Perfections of Jesus

(Matthew 27:3-4; Luke 23:41; 2 Corinthians 5:21; Hebrews 2:10; Isaiah 53:9; 2 Timothy 2:13)

Copeland speaks outrageous and astonishing things against the Lord of the Lords and King of Kings—Jesus Christ. You cannot deny this, with him called Jesus an *"emaciated (poured out) little wormy spirit"* who is suffering at Satan's hand *"down in the bottom of that thing (the pit of hell)."* Then, he compounds this blasphemy by saying that Jesus took on the nature of Satan! This is the kind of astonishing blasphemy of which the Bible foretells, as it warns of the coming Antichrist! Listen:

"And the king shall do according to his will; he shall exalt himself and magnify himself above every god and shall speak astonishing things against the God of gods and shall prosper till the indignation be accomplished..." [Daniel 11:36; Parallel Bible, KJV/Amplified Bible Commentary]

Notice that Jesus will not immediately strike such a person dead when he speaks astonishing things against Him, but will actually allow him to "prosper" until "the indignation be accomplished". Today, Copeland, Hagan, Hinn and Crouch of TBN are all prospering, as the money continues to flow in to the organization in copious quantities; but do not be misled into believing that the very presence of the wealth of TBN means that God is present and pleased. No, He is simply allowing the "indignation be accomplished". Then, judgment will flow at the proper time, the time of God's own choosing.

Transcribed From Trinity Broadcasting Networks Praise The Lord Show: Yet More Blasphemy

The Deity Of Man And The Teaching That We Are "Little Gods"

Let's go straight to several statements by Paul Crouch, Benny Hinn, and Kenneth Copeland on this crucial subject. After seeing the denial of Jesus Christ's eternal divinity, it is amazing to hear them elevate man unto a "god" status. From Praise The Lord Show:

Paul Crouch: "He doesn't ever draw a distinction between himself." (Jan Crouch agrees in the background.)
Kenneth Copeland: "Never, never. You never can do that in a covenant relationship."
Paul Crouch: "You know what else that settles then tonight. This hue and cry and controversy that has been spawned by the devil to try and bring dissent within the body of Christ that we are gods. *I am a little god.*"
Kenneth Copeland: "*Yes, yes!*"

Paul Crouch: "I have His name. I'm one with Him. I'm in a covenant relationship. *I am a little god."*
Kenneth Copeland: "Critic, *you are anything that He is."*
Paul Crouch (heard under the worth of Kenneth Copeland): "Critic, be gone."
Paul Crouch: "Yes!" [Emphasis added]

Until reading this quote, I thought only Satanists and New Age adherents believed that all people are "little gods" within. The reason for the occult path is to make it possible for the adherent to steadily and through many steps, "realize his own godhood" that has been with him for all this time. Of course, since the Preacher has told us there is "nothing new under the Sun" [Ecclesiastes 1:9], we must realize this "little gods" belief goes straight back to Satan's original lie to Eve in the Garden of Eden, when he told her—

"For God doth know that in the day ye eat thereof, then your eyes shall be opened, and ye shall be as gods..." [Gen 3:5]

Transcribed From Trinity Broadcasting Networks Praise The Lord Show.

Benny Hinn: "Adam was a superbeing when God created Him. I don't know whether people even know this, but he was the first superman that ever lived. (Jan Crouch is heard laughing on the set.) First of all, the Scriptures declare clearly that he had dominion over the fowls of the air, the fish of the sea, which means he used to fly."
Jan Crouch: "Wow!"
Benny Hinn: "Of course, how can you have dominion over the birds and not be able to do what they do?"
Jan Crouch: "Whoa, I mean, wait a minute. Benny, wait a minute."
Benny Hinn: "I'll prove it to you. The word 'dominion' in the Hebrew clearly declares that, if you have dominion over a subject, you can do everything that subject does. In other words, that subject, if it does something that you cannot do, you don't have

dominion over it. I'll prove it further. Adam not only flew, he flew to space. He used to be...He,He,He,He,He,He...with one thought He'd be on the moon."

Benny Hinn may have uttered this complete nonsense, content with the knowledge that his listeners did not even know their Bibles, not to mention know how to do a word study using Strongs and other study resources. Let us review Strong's Concordance on the Hebrew meaning of the word, 'dominion', found in Genesis 1:26.

Dominion—Strong's Number 7287—Transliteration: radah—Phonetic Pronunciation: raw-daw'

Meaning: to rule, have dominion, dominate, tread down—1a) (Qal) to have dominion, rule, subjugate—1b) (Hiphil) to cause to dominate—2) to scrape out as honey out of a hive—2a) (Qal) to scrape, scrape out

The ways in which this word is used in the Bible: rule 13—dominion 9—take 2—prevaileth 1—reign 1—ruler 1—[Total Count: 27]

Now, let us turn to the Key Word Hebrew/Greek Study Bible. Listen to what they say about the meaning of "dominion—radah: To tread down as a winepress, with the feet; to subdue, subjugate, to crumble, oppress, to walk on a person, to rule, cause to rule, to prevail against, to take possession of honey from a hive, to scrape out. [Page 1659]

Can you see any definition of "radah" that suggests that the person exercising the control over the birds "can do everything that subject does"? What sheer nonsense Benny Hinn is shoveling out to his gullible crowd of followers! He pretends to know Hebrew just because he claims to be Jewish. That is about as logical as a person claiming to speak German just because he is of German descent.

Adam Was a Reproduction of God Himself?

Copeland: "God's reason for creating Adam was His desire to reproduce Himself and in the Garden of Eden, He did that, He was not a little like God, He was not almost like God, he was subordinate to God, even. And Adam was as much like God as you can get…And I want you to know something. Adam in the Garden of Eden was God manifested In the flesh."

Once again, this "new revelation" is sheer nonsense, and totally unbiblical! God simply said, "Let us make man in our image…" [Genesis 1:26] This word, "image" is "tselem", which literally means likeness, resemblance, illusion, a phantom, nothingness." {Key Study Bible, Hebrew/Greek, p. 1653]

In other words, God made man as a faint phantom of His true Self. While God granted unto man the intellectual ability to know right from wrong and to solve problems, He never made man exactly like He was; man was never, ever a "little god", and never, ever a "reproduction" of God.

Does The Scripture Teach The "Little God" Concept?

The answer is obviously, "No!" There are many great truths of Scripture that show our humanity and the hope of a future glorification.

> - *Presently, We Are Tempted*— *"My brethren, count It all joy when ye fall into divers temptations; Knowing this, that the trying of your faith worketh patience."* (James 1:2-3).

> - *Our Outward Man Perisheth*— *"For which cause we faint not; but though our outward man perish, yet the inward {man] is renewed day by day."* (II Corinthians 4:16).

> - *Our Hope Is At The Completion Of Our Earthly Journey*— *"Wherefore gird up the loins of your mind, be sober, and hope to the end for the grace that is to be brought unto you at the revelation of Jesus Christ."* (1 Peter 1:13).

It is certainly clear that this entire TBN concept is a cheap path to riches and earthly glory. To look for some spiritual benefit in this false doctrine is a total waste of time. The purpose of this false teaching is to create a whole class of "swinging saints living the good life", something akin to the "Beverly Hillbillies". You would think this crowd has been watching too much television. When you look at the real Jesus of Scripture, the prophets and apostles in their suffering and sacrifice, and then return to see Paul and Jan and their fellow travelers in their materialism, it all becomes a flimsy fantasy world of deception. However, flimsy though this deception is to a person thoroughly familiar with Biblical Doctrine, many millions of people worldwide are falling for this spiritual deception, a deception that will lead them directly into an eternal Hell.

Is God Both Male And Female? Androgynous?

The pagan roots of this whole deception are manifest as TBN creates a God who becomes more like Zeus and the pantheon of ancient gods. I have been aware for some time that this entire theological confusion was headed back to its pagan roots. These men and women are clever, but they will eventually become so deluded that their error will show through. Listen as Kenneth Copeland clearly states God is both male and female. Next, listen to Benny Hinn state that women were first created to bear children out of their side; then, he somehow compares this to Jesus and the spear print in His side.

> Copeland: "Then, he created Eve out of Adam. Now, actually God didn't name her Eve, Adam named her Eve later. That wasn't her name, her name was Adam-Adam. When God said Adam, they both came. Their authority was one and the same together. They did everything together. They had always been together. Even when she was still part of him, he was as much female as he was male, LIKE GOD IS. And God separated the female part of him and then put them back together. And she was Adam, they were Adam. He was the man, she was the woman. She was the man with the womb."

In one brief moment, Kenneth Copeland took TBN directly into very dangerous pagan waters, as he teaches that God created Adam and Eve as androgynous beings,. i.e., having both male and female characteristics. Remember our earlier assertion that the theology of TBN and the Crouch's are Greek in nature? In the first paragraph of this section, we mentioned that the 'God' of TBN was more like Zeus of the Greek pantheon. This teaching is straight out of Zeus. Did you know that, in the Zeus mythology, many beings were androgynous? Listen to one author explain:

> "In closing I will quote from Plato on what humans once were. It is not actually a belief in origins but in the origins of loneliness and love. Here is the edited speech at the Banquet by Aristophanes (189e-193b of Plato's Symposium):
>
> "Anciently...the androgynous sex existed...coupled back to back...till jealous Jupiter divided then vertically...as people cut eggs with hairs...after then, these divided and imperfect folk ran about over the earth ever seeking their lost halves to be joined to them again...and the reason being that human nature was originally one, and the desire and pursuit of the whole is called love...." [http://www.mythome.org/greekorigins.html]

Therefore, Copeland is simply offering a slightly modified version of Plato's lie that Adam and Eve were androgynous originally and were separated by Jupiter, creating an "imperfect race". Copeland modified this teaching simply by saying that Adam and Eve were independently androgynous. Let us examine another source to get yet another aspect of Greek mythology relating to Zeus and androgynous humans.

> "Hermaphroditus) Greek androgynous deity. The cult of Hermaphroditos appeared first in Cyprus...Originally the son of Hermes and Aphrodite. The Naiad Salmakis (associated with a fountain of the same name in Caria, a region of Anatolia) fell so passionately in love with him that their bodies merged into one. In some versions, it was her entreaties to the gods that finally resulted

in their becoming one being." [http://mrugala.free.fr/Religions/Divers/Anglais/Gofhe.htm]

This next quote tells you why the Greeks held the androgynous deity in the highest esteem:

"Athena is an odd mixture of both the male and female, yet she is widely loved and accepted by the Greeks...Her aspect as the goddess of wisdom and Zeus' counselor also shows her androgynous position, as she represents both the male and female, impartial in her justice, resolute in her support...Athena is an icon, an ideal of virgin perfection; she is a fusion of the martial and intellectual that exemplifies the best of the ancient Greek civilization." [http://www.titan.spaceports.com/~neogeo/athena.html]

Greeks viewed the male/female ideal—androgyny—as representing the best characteristics possible because such a union represents the "fusion of the martial and intellectual". As we stated at the top of this article, TBN is "Christian in name without being Christian in theology"; now, we can see that TBN is actually Greek in theology! That is serious, because the greatest Greek leader of all time was Alexander the Great, a type of Antichrist.

Now, let us examine yet one more instance of pagan philosophy as Benny Hinn continues to expound:

"Holy Spirit said something to me and I had to go like a mad man and looking in the Word. He says, 'God's original plan is that the woman was to bring forth children out her other side.' What? You know that there is nowhere in the Bible but where God gives birth out of His side? Jesus gives birth to the church out of His side. Adam gives birth to his wife out of his side. It was sin that turned the thing around. And it was sin that transformed her flesh and her body."

Such an idea is certainly blasphemous. It is exactly the same foolishness that elevates Mary, the mother of Jesus to the state of "The Mother of God."

Many writers are beginning to suggest, as Copeland, that God has a dual nature of male and female. The entire new headquarters of Trinity Broadcasting Network is feminine in design. There are female angels guarding the entrance to the television studio. The ceilings are filled with frolicking, mostly nude children. Two pictures of the mother/child deception and one with a feminine face, with two nude young bodies hovering above, line the short hallway leading past the female angels to the studio. The appearance is mythological and pagan, and most definitely not Christian!

The Bible is absolutely clear that God is our Heavenly Father. His nature is divine and eternal and sexual distinctions are non-existent. He created man in His image and then created woman. There are no female angels because the angelic host were created in the image of God before women were created. Women are a unique creation out of man to supply him a help-meet and have absolutely nothing to do with the nature and appearance of God. This false concept of God being both male and female is clearly descending into rank paganism.

God As 'Mother Nature'

As TBN moves to the pagan concept of a dual nature, male and female, supposedly manifest in the Heavenly Father, the results can only lead to more disgusting ideas. The new additional studio of Trinity Broadcasting Network in Hendersonville, TN, is the scene of the following quotes. Jan Crouch appears to be the host of these events, with preachers like Phil Munsey and Kim Clement. On one occasion Phil is preaching and appears to be speaking more from "fertility rites of ancient paganism" than the Bible itself. He states:

> "There is going to be a paradigm shift in philosophies of men. Mother Earth is 'groaning in travail', laboring pain, ready to give birth to something big and something mighty and wonderful...God is moving—connect with Him."

As he preaches, he mentions the Buddhists and directs his remarks to them. "Buddhists, I love you much, I'm honored that you are willing to get out of yourself and take a risk and go for something that people used to laugh at. I'm honored that you have enough passion for God to try to connect with something."

This teaching is extremely New Age, so much so that it merges effortlessly and seamlessly into the occult teaching that is preparing the hearts and minds of hundreds of millions of people today for Antichrist. New Age teachers began to preach a "paradigm shift" back in the mid-1970's, by which they meant that a sudden, mighty shift in attitudes and values was about to occur that would allow the New Age "Christ" to appear. Likewise, the word "connect" is very common with the occult as it represents the union of man and the 'gods', i.e., demonic gods.

TBN is leading its followers directly into the arms of the coming Antichrist!

> Phil Munsey: "In the Throne Zone, time past, present, and future cease to exist. We move into a frame without the limitation of humanity in the natural."

In the course of these several nights of so-called revival, he apparently tried to show that people in the heathen world have learned how to connect with the principles of "God" without being Christians. I presume this is why he spoke so kindly of the Buddhist. Listen:

> Phil Munsey: "People learn how to work the principles of God, they learn how to operate in the charisma of God without the character of God and that makes good people mad."

This pagan teaching will get you right into Hell, for if you strive to "operate in the charisma of God" while consciously eschewing the "character of God", you are going straight to the Abyss, because no one, but no one, ever enters into the Kingdom of Heaven without the character of God being imputed to him or her from Jesus Christ. That is the symbolism of wearing the white robes; Jesus said no one would enter Heaven without His white robe, His white and shining and pure wedding dress. Listen:

> *"...when the king came in to see the guests, he saw there a man which had not on a wedding garment: And he saith unto him, Friend, how camest thou in hither not having a wedding garment? And he was speechless. Then said the king to the servants, Bind him hand and foot, and take him away, and cast him into outer darkness; there shall be weeping and gnashing of teeth."*
> [Matt 22:11-13]

The phrase, "weeping and gnashing of teeth" is clearly Hell. No one enters Heaven without the imputed character, righteousness, of Jesus God.

Phil Munsey: "Get your ears to hear what the Spirit says now, Get your ear to hear what the Spirit says now. (Supposedly, the Spirit is speaking through him.) I tell you that the kingdom of God is so due and overdue. I tell you that Mother Nature and I don't mind using that word. . . It is now time for the New Jerusalem to come down out of heaven and kiss the earth until all that God is shall be made known and His glory fills the earth.. . I tell you what God is going to, has to do. He's either going to shut some mouths up that are aborting the purpose of God and bring some marriages...If you are a virgin and you are telling people you are pregnant, you could get stoned."

Phil Munsey: "God is looking for a womb to bring forth Rhenna upon the earth. The Bible says in Isaiah, chapter 34:16, and I love the Amplified Version, that "everything in nature has a mate of which they bring forth from their seed . . . Every Word of God has a mate..."

What a terrible twisting of Scripture! The Amplified Bible Commentary does NOT say that "everything in nature has a mate...Every Word of God has a mate". What the verse does say is that each Prophecy of God will receive a mate in the fulfillment of that prophecy! Listen:

> *"Seek out of the book of the Lord and read: not one of these [details of prophecy] shall fail, none shall want and lack her mate [in fulfillment]. For the mouth [of the Lord] has commanded, and His Spirit has gathered them."*

Let God's Word be true and every false prophet like Munsey be found a liar!

Can Truth Of Scripture Be Blended With Pagan Doctrines?

The answer is obviously a resounding, "No!" When God the Father becomes "mother god" as much as "father god", anything becomes possible in the pulpit. The term Mother Earth, as used by Munsey on these TBN Broadcasts suggests that the occultic paradigm shift has reached an intense level of change within this so-called Christian movement. These doctrines will be preached very carefully for awhile and then the speakers will grow blatant and arrogant.

Notice that Munsey says that the Spirit was saying, "the kingdom of God is so due and overdue?" The wording of this statement implies that God's plan is late, and may be approaching the failure stage. Is God ever late? Does He have to apologize for the "failure" of His plan? Copeland has already answered that on an earlier 'Praise The Lord; telecast. "God," says Copeland, "was the biggest Failure ever in history."

Antichrist paganism has arrived at the pulpits of these churches.

Standing On The Infallible, Eternal, Unchanging Word Of God—The Eternal Anchor of Your Soul

My dear friends, get back to the truth of God's Eternal Word with all of your heart. Israel was experiencing much of this type of pagan revival, and had gone spiritually lusting after pagan idols rather than the Eternal God whom their forefathers had seen work mightily in their midst. Just before God sent physical destructive judgment that destroyed Israel, He pleaded:

"Thus saith the LORD, Stand ye in the ways, and see, and ask for the old paths, where is the good way, and walk therein, and ye shall find rest for your souls." [Jer 6:16]

Whenever you hear a person ridicule the "old paths" of God's Word, or tell you not to allow "traditions" to stand in your way, get up and leave that church so quickly the door will not hit you on the way out! That person is a false prophet.

Biblical Truth will set you free. Do not allow these "New Wave" preachers force you to deny the beautiful ministry of the Holy Spirit in your life. The Holy Spirit was sent by the Father as the Spirit of truth. His living presence in the church will cause the Word of God to come alive in your heart, full of power and bringing joy. My heart is set on a reformation in the Body of Christ. The church world has a multitude of sincere believers who love the eternal Son of Cod, but many of them have been influenced by these pagan ideas. Pray earnestly for the "Word of God to prevail." Let's be sure that each one of us gets back into total Biblical truth and prays for a revival of genuine New Testament Christianity.

Pray earnestly for the Crouches, and others, that truth will prevail in their lives. Millions are being led into deeper and deeper error and everyone of us has an obligation to help them learn the truth. Share this information with everybody in your sphere of influence. As you survey this entire Charismatic Confusion, led by Kenneth Hagin, Benny Hinn, Paul and Jan Crouch, Kenneth Copeland, and others within the TBN network, you can appreciate the huge height, depth, and width of the unprecedented spiritual and political deception running rampant in the churches of today [Matthew 24:24]

While the world is at least one thousands years away from the New Jerusalem coming down out of heaven, we seem to be getting close to the appearance of Antichrist. And, the "Christian church" is opening the door to him![33]

CHAPTER 7

SPECTATOR SPORT

"Old-Time Religion"

"America means far more than a continent bounded by two oceans. It is more than pride of military power, glory in war, or in victory. It means more than vast expanses of farms, of great factories or mines, magnificent cities or millions of automobiles, radios, and televisions. It is more than even the great tide westward from Europe which pioneered the conquest of a continent. The meaning of America flows from one pure spring. The soul of our America is its freedom of mind and spirit in man. Here alone are the windows through which pours the sunlight of the human spirit. Here alone is human dignity, not a dream, but an accomplishment."

—Herbert Hoover

Can you remember the general stores with potbellied stoves, pickle barrels and penny candy, the open fires where corn was popped and marshmallows were toasted, the fish fries and berry-picking times, hayrides and caroling, the sweetness of autumn apples, lazy summer days and Indian summer in October? When Americans gave a days' work for a days' pay, spent less than they earned, and asked the same of their government. You went to church, your children to Sunday School, discipline and education went hand-in-hand. This America of yesterday became prosperous and secure, rebuilt from a shattering depression and claimed victory in two World Wars. Her people became the most fortunate on earth, and were proud of the red, the white, and the blue. When your neighbor's barn burned down, you and everyone else were there to help and rebuild it. I wouldn't count on such benevolence today; neighbors hardly even speak anymore. The family doctor, in times past, made house calls and was happy to leave with a ham or turkey, now he wants the whole hog and most of your chickens as payment. I often hear on the news that the economy is improving—whose economy are they talking about?

The quaint churches of rural America generally had neither tall steeples, nor stained glass windows, and most were in need for a coat of paint and numerous other cosmetic face-lifts. Humble souls, mostly dressed in work clothes, ushered quietly inside to worship their Savior and fellowship one with the other. Yes, this is the church, God's people, built with the blood and tears of the early Pilgrims, who endured persecution and suffered loss of material possessions. These pioneer Christians gathered with common, unselfish goals, shared all things equally, and grew in strength and character.

People, not so long ago, prayed for the burdens of one another, shared concerns, and recurrently their fortunes. There was little bitterness in the flock, and pride, well there wasn't enough to go around. Air conditioning was not needed to cool off hot tempers, while the umbrella of love remained sufficient, had Christ at the head and lived as sheep in the fold. Elegant buildings erode with time and are demolished for progress, but the Spirit lives on and endures forever.

Nearly forty years ago as a young lad I can remember my dad taking me to tent revivals. They were similar to the "big top" at the circus, a huge tent with sawdust spread over the ground. The vast majority of worshippers came in everyday garments, casual and very comfortable, wearing a friendly smile and excited about hearing good preaching—not professional, just good.

Hell-fire and brimstone echoed from the pulpit accompanied with congregational singing, and with no boundary of time, we could start all over again and continue indefinitely. Plain folks who could not have made a public speech or won a fashion contest would become overjoyed—praising God and shaking hands throughout the congregation. These old-fashioned revivals and tent meetings had their faults, but they were genuine, not imitators of the "real McCoy," and when the audience sang acappella, mostly off-key, justice was served on many of the old favorites. Legitimate hymns that were not costumed to the likeness of gospel jazz or hootenannies.

"And all that believed were together, and had all things common; and sold their possessions and goods, and parted them to all men, as every man had need. And they, continuing daily with one accord in the temple, and breaking bread from house to house, did eat their meat with gladness and singleness of heart, praising God, and having favor with all people."
—Acts 2:44-47

"When peace, like a river attendeth my way, When sorrows like sea billows roll— Whatever my lot, Thou hast taught me to say, It is well, it is well with my soul."
—Horatio Spafford

The evening service was merely a continuation of the morning worship, with honest preaching, more singing, babies crying, and ordinary folks enjoying "Beulah Land." Such revivals have been burlesqued and made the subject of jests that approach sacrilege, but there was one colossal difference between them and the imitators of today: they were bona fide.

"I am an old-fashioned preacher of the old-time religion, that has warmed this cold world's heart for two thousand years."
—Billy Sunday

It was great when public education was founded and gave all Americans and their children an equal opportunity. America became the world leader in technology, medicine, and science; our pioneering and engineering cut in-roads and avenues into virtually every known field. Today, however, nearly 15% of Americans are illiterate, while colleges continue to lower test scores on entrance exams to maintain the status quo. The experts say that laziness is the primary reason, for people simply want more than they are willing to work for and earn. As a nation we spend more than our income, and on numerous occasions will even sacrifice our families in order to achieve a certain amount of notoriety. "Gold-bricking," "brown-nosing," and "sexual favors," have gone a great distance in degrading our economic and social system. A spineless society does not fail politically—ultimately it fails spiritually.

> "Lord, with glowing heart I'd praise Thee,
> For the bliss Thy love bestows,
> For the pardoning grace that saves me,
> And the peace that from it flows;
> Help, O God, my weak endeavor;
> This dull soul to rapture raise;
> Thou must light the flame or never
> Can my love be warmed to praise."
> —Francis Scott Key

"Our Modern Institution"

"We believe whatever we want to believe."
—Demosthenes, 348 B.C.

"We are being born to believe, and if no church comes forward with all the title-deeds of truth, and sustained by the tradition of sacred ages and the conviction of countless generations to guide us, we will find altars and idols in our own heart and imagination."
—Benjamin Disraeli

We shall now examine the flip side of this coin and delve into the fabrication and character of our modern day churches—these twentieth century wonders exhibited across the land.

The modern cathedral with its acquired corporeal properties lodged high on a hill, stained glass windows that glisten in the sunlight, monuments adorn the exterior, and chimes summoning parishioners to worship. Inside this magnificent edifice we observe padded pews, flowing purple drapes, and ornamental fixtures, with the hundreds of worshippers parading their "Sunday's best" attire across plush red carpet, swaying to the vibrations of costly musical instruments. Does this sound familiar to most of you? These architectural wonders that traverse our domain are enticing indeed, but is this the "true church?" It would be well to remember that most frequently, "with riches, come sorrows."

> *"Let your days be Mine to order;*
> *Where I lead, obedient be.*
> *Let your own desires be nothing;*
> *Only seek to follow Me."*
> —Anonymous

Many of our churches, America's heritage, have left her first love and begun to walk down that lasting Roman Road of destruction. Her clergy have been caught up in these inflationary times and as a result concocted various gimmicks and numerous gadgets to keep the machine works mobile. The church has turned to an idol called "materialism" and bathed herself in an orgy of "secular humanism." What will the end result be?

> *"He that hath an ear, let him hear what the*
> *Spirit saith unto the churches. And unto the angel of the church of the Laodiceans write;*
> *These things saith the Amen, the faithful and true witness, the beginning of the creation of God. I know thy works, that thou art neither cold nor hot: I would thou was cold or hot. So then because thou art lukewarm, and neither cold nor hot, I will spew thee out of my mouth.*
> *Because thou sayest, I am rich, and increased with goods, and have need of nothing; and knowest not that thou art wretched, and*
> *miserable, and poor, and blind, and naked."*
> —Revelation 3:13-17

There is one very important ingredient absent in the church today—purity: a cleansing from sin and all unrighteousness, an ingredient necessary to preserve unity and uphold honesty. God's people must set aside time for self-examination, for house-cleaning, and an outcry for church discipline. Our revivals and evangelism have become shallow and superficial producing poor ground for any real cultivation. We rededicate ourselves to death on Sunday, but on Monday it's the flesh and the devil all over again.

> *"If my people, which are called by my name, shall humble themselves, and pray, and seek my face, and turn from their wicked ways; then will I hear from heaven, and will forgive their sin, and will heal their land."*
> —II Chronicles 7:14

Several years ago a prominent middle-aged couple—who were once very active in church affairs—found it necessary to start attending services again and renew some prior commitments. She was searching for answers to life's questions, while he pursued other female companionship—being an above average baritone joined the church choir, and soon began making eyes at the second alto. She, too, was married, however, this did not change the ending of the story. Eventually the minister became involved with both families, but never once was church discipline conducted and both remained in the choir because the preacher considered them an asset to the music program.

A great number of other churches have grown too large for proper Biblical cleansing; to carry out Christ's command for purity would be virtually impossible. However, ignoring these commands of our Lord could result in spiritual sickness and physical death within the rank and file.

> "In the name of our Lord Jesus Christ, when you are gathered together, and my spirit, with the power of our Lord Jesus Christ, to deliver such a one unto Satan for the destruction of the flesh, that the spirit may be saved in the day of the Lord Jesus. Your glorying is not good. Know you not that a little leaven leaveneth the whole lump? Purge out therefore the old leaven, that you may be a new lump, as you are unleavened. For even Christ our passover is sacrificed for us: therefore let us keep the feast, not with old leaven, neither with the leaven of malice and wickedness; but with the unleavened bread of sincerity and truth."
> —I Corinthians 5:4-8

These are lawless times with little regard for authority, and thus, pierced our genial atmosphere at about the same pace as in the political and social segments of our society. Because our nation was born and nurtured on religious freedom, "one nation under God," we stand to be judged more severely. Religion that was once a person's life—and often death—is commonly practiced today as a higher form of culture; penetrated with ungodliness and immorality.

Church membership is still at an extremely high level, yet our family life and ethical standards are rapidly declining, and worst of all our children are being forfeited to Eastern philosophies and humanistic concepts. Our leaders of tomorrow have lost faith in the system. With impurity and sacrilege being tolerated, discipline faltering, and the "new morality" code of ethics, many church members have become blinded and complacent. Prevalent lusts and sins are corroding the very foundations of our religious system; the superstructure will inevitably fall with no spiritual backbone to hold it together. Listen well to what the Apostle Jude foresaw about the church of today—our modern institution.

> "For there are certain men crept in unawares, who were before of old ordained to this condemnation, ungodly men, turning the grace of our God into lasciviousness, and denying the only Lord God, and our Lord Jesus Christ."
> —Jude 4

> "In actual living, and in its deepest sense, your religion is the fundamental way you approach, understand and evaluate all subjects. It consists of your first principles, the truths you regard as self-evident, the basic axioms you take for granted, and through which you view everything else. Your religion colors your outlook upon the universe, affecting the way you look upon life, your relation to other people, your treatment of things."
> —Edmund A. Optiz

Our most guarded televised worship services present a distorted view of eschatology today. They give the impressions that walking down aisles, being baptized, wearing or displaying ornaments, or joining a particular denomination will inevitably put one on good terms with the God of the universe. This twisted view of health, wealth, and happiness is "pulpit psychology" aimed at lining the pockets of the rank and file, and their ministries.

Trinity Broadcasting Network (TBN) is the largest religious programming network in the world. Its host, Paul Crouch, has a boutique look, his wife Jan is glamorized by bleached wigs. The thrust of TBN's heart and soul, employs and embraces the charismatic movement—the fastest growing religious transition of ideals in America today. The charismatics encompass a "name it, claim it theology" that appeals to the upper middle class segment in society; while, the "speaking in tongues" fantasy is comprised largely by the female gender because of the emotion involved.

Charismatic views are anti-intellectual, a quasimystical approach to understanding. These people for the most part would kiss the toes of gurus or engage in various other mystical or eastern philosophies if the feeling was there. They want a "quick fix", a cheap entrance to God and Holy Living.

> "The life of fellowship with God cannot be built up in a day. It begins with the habitual reference of all to Him, hour by hour. It then moves on to more and longer periods of communion; and it finds its consummation and bliss in days and nights of intercession and waiting."
>
> —F.B. Meyer

The entertainers on TBN are a prime example of modern Christian talent and testimony in religious broadcasting today. Their occasional jigs along with the singing and music portrays the true message endorsed by the network. The only difference between Trinity Music City in Hendersonville and Nashville on Stage is an apparent shortage for a horse and saddle. Many of the other regulars portray that "pampered look," everything concentrating on the outward appearance with little or no spiritual depth. Their big bellies, dangling earrings, and diamond watches are nourished and purchased with your hard earned money. God help our meager endeavors.

> "Whether therefore you eat, or drink, or whatsoever you do, do all to the glory of God."
> —I Corinthians 10:31

"Willow Creek"

Willow Creek Community Church located on the outskirts of Chicago is one of the best-attended churches in America. Seventeen thousand gather every Sunday to enjoy a theatrical performance of "feel good" religion. Loud music, flashing lights, actors, and a huge stage, led one member to say: "It's like going to a movie, only better."

Then, why do people go to movies? The only reasonable answer is to get entertained and to escape from reality; not in tune with God or spirituality. Mystical religions seek to escape from reality, and they achieve it in a less dramatic fashion. The bottom line, then, for Willow Creek Community Church is carnal and commercial- not spiritual. Church Incorporated—the marketing agent for the church—operates on the edge of hell!

What is the bottom line? Willow Creek—and how many others like it—is a showboat of a church to the world. The church serves up music that is likened to drugs and alcohol—intoxicating, deceptive, and destructive. God's church was never intended to meet the world's standards.

> *"That very church which the world likes best is sure to be that which God abhors."*
> —C. H. Spurgeon

> *"Lighthouses don't toot horns; they just shine."*
> —Dwight L. Moody

"Contemporary Christian Rock"

The fastest growing music in the world is Christian Rock—an epidemic in our land. It is neither Christian, nor Rock—an insult to both. People who have left the mainstream religions are greatly attracted to this "Jesus Music"; where the words and the beat are both heretical and unholy. Christian Rock sugar-coats the gospel and waters downs Biblical principles in words and vibrations that captivates the audience.

This unremitting, palpitating, syncopated rhythm deploys the worshipper into a hypnotic state and causes him or her to lose active control over their conscious minds. The bottom beat on the bass guitar and the incessant sound of the drums in all actuality has proximity to voodoo and pagan worship, with the message being lost in the midst of the music. Entertainers are able to channel the music and direct it into communication with the body and not the soul.

"Christian Rockers" resemble a tragic case of worldly-mindedness. They like both the music and the message. It presents a rush from reality and solitude into a frenzic state of thunderous noise and uncontrolled hand-waving. These charismatics are mere throw-backs to their high school pep-rally days.

"Raucous Christian rock dares to challenge the overall message of Scripture. We have been created to have fellowship with God. This means that we are to be good listeners. We must be 'still' to know. Though God created the beauty of music for our enjoyment and pleasure, it should never replace the wonder of the quiet moments in His presence. Our Father desires that we love Him, unaided by anything but our soul's deepest desire. I submit to you that the punk-rockin' professing Christian groups are not leading believers in this direction. We cannot even understand what they are singing about because of their elusive enunciation."[34]

> *"Be still, and know that I am God: I will be exalted among the heathen, I will be exalted in the earth."*
> —Psalm 46:10

"So-called" Christian artists are ninety-nine percent phony. They are in it for the fame and fortune—mostly the fortune. The following are two prime examples:

Sandi Patti

Sandi Patti is the highest paid Gospel entertainer in the world, averaging $75,000 for a two-hour performance (Don Cusic, Sandi Patti, (New York, 1988), pp. 211-212) (not to mention profits from T-shirts, records, etc). At $37,000 an hour, who is Sandi Patti really serving? God or mammon? Jesus Christ said in Matthew 6:24, "No man can serve two masters: for either he will hate the one, and love the other...Ye cannot serve God and mammon."

Sandi's album, *LeVoyage*, is so rock oriented *CCM Magazine* (May 93 p.40) says "...old-line Patti fans are either going to be seeking refunds in droves, or be so flabbergasted at seeing an entirely new side of her..." And of course, the wonderful name of Jesus is nowhere to be found.

Out of over 2000 words the name of Jesus is nowhere to be found! What do these so-called Christian stars have against the wonderful name of Jesus? You would think a real Christian would want to tell the whole world about Jesus!

What a difference from the disciples (some REAL Christians) in Acts 5:42 says, " And daily in the temple, and in every house, they ceased not to teach and preach Jesus Christ."

According to Christianity Today (September 11, 1995 pp. 72-74) Sandi Patti was committing adultery with Don Pesli as far back as 1991! And the article (p. 72) also stated that, "According to several independent sources who at different times were aware of Patti's activities, she took part in two extramarital relationships, in both cases with married men." A large part of Sandi Patti's career she was committing adultery with married men! How could the Holy Spirit possibly bless her music!

Rather than do what the Bible commands (after all, what's the Bible got to do with it...) and get her previous marriage right with God, as her first husband wanted, Sandi's adulterous appetite "wrecked" two families. And on August 6, 1995, after divorcing her first husband, she married Don Peslis. No wonder the name of Jesus wasn't on her last albums! Anyone living in such gross sin would have a hard time singing about sinless Jesus! 2 Timothy 2:19, "...Let every one that nameth the name of Christ depart from iniquity."

PsychoHeresy Awareness Letter gives the following Biblical analysis of Sandi's lying and adultery:

A recent *World* magazine article (September 16, 1995) states:

Ms. Patti, who claims to have been in counseling since 1989, attributes her pattern of "keeping secrets" to her childhood molestation, the memory of which she recovered in therapy.

The article reveals that prior to her divorce Patti was already involved in an adulterous relationship with Don Peslis, a former backup singer. Patti and Peslis both divorced their spouses and are now married. According to a *Christianity Today* article (October 23, 1995, p. 89), "Patti also admitted to another adulterous relationship."

The subtitle of the *World* magazine article is: "Gospel singer Sandi Patti confesses to adulterous affair." The title of the article is "She did it her way." Yes, she certainly "did it her way," but it was not God's way. God's way is not committing adultery or lying; nor is it God's way to destroy two families and to stand as a horrible testimony to the world and to the children involved.

Psychotherapy may have made her feel better about herself while disobeying God and destroying her family. It may have given her some bogus excuses at the time. And, perhaps it's helping her rationalize the pain she has caused others. But. that's not God's way. (*PsychoHeresy Awareness Letter*, Nov.-Dec. 1995 p.8)

Combine the sinful heart with the sinful flesh and you have the adultery and lying that have characterized Sandi Patti's life...

Patti's rising popularity is indicative of the trashed condition of Christians who claim the name of Christ but will not follow the doctrines of the Bible. Marrying a partner in adultery does not make the relationship right. It constitutes a continual condition of disobedience to God. How does one repent of adultery while one continues in an ongoing relationship with a former accomplice in adultery? Sin is further compounded while it festers under the lackly sanctions of a compromised institution...by God's standards Sandi Patti simply moved from adultery into a sinful divorce and then into marriage with her adultery partner, who divorced his wife. (*PsychoHeresy Awareness Letter*, March-April 1998 pp.1, 8)[35]

Michael English

In 1994, Michael English swept the Gospel Music Association's Dove awards, winning six awards, including the prestigious artist of the year. But a few days later, English confessed to an affair with Marabeth Jordon of the Christian rock trio First Call. When their "pleasures of sin for a season" (see Heb. 11:25) was over—two families lay in ruins. And how did Michael English respond to his "caught in the act"? Did English show any Christ-honoring-repentance? Not hardly—he's opening for the secular group Foreigner! By the way, have you seen the cover of Michael English's post-adultery album? With long hair, and goat-tee, a la Nirvana—the look of rebellion is openly flaunted.

People say, *"Yea, but look at David's sin"*. *Yea, but look at David's repentance!* Just read Psalms 51, 51:1-3 *"Have mercy upon me, O God, according to thy lovingkindness: according unto the multitude of thy tender mercies blot out my transgressions. Wash me thoroughly from mine iniquity, and cleanse me from my sin. For I acknowledge my transgressions: and my sin is ever before me.* Compare that to Sandi Patti having not one, but two extramarital affairs for several years, and after "getting caught" rather than putting her previous marriage back together, she marries her "partner in crime". And English forsaking Christians and opening for secular-lustful Foreigner!

Jesus says in Matthew 7:20, *"Wherefore by their fruits ye shall know them.*[36]

"The Falwell Faux Pas: Another Towering Inferno"

The following article is printed with permission by Paul Proctor.

I'm sure many evangelicals squirmed in their seats as they watched Jerry Falwell trying to save himself on ABC's Good

Morning America by claiming he didn't really mean what he said the day before on Pat Robertson's 700 Club about homosexuals and abortionists being responsible for the twin towers tragedy. Fortunately, I didn't witness either performance, but was nonetheless saddened by the accounts I read of his awkward attempt at covering one embarrassing faux pas with another.

As much as we would like, mainstream America and its media are never going to accept the fact that disobedience to God has dire consequences. Don't expect to hear any network news anchor admit to their audience that the "wages of sin is death". By the same token, Christians should understand that any effort they make to fence-straddle their way into the limelight is going to end in a disaster. It is foolish to think that befriending the world with flattery and compromise, "for the sake of the gospel", as Jerry Falwell and others like him so often try to do, will make them anything but a casualty in the culture's own crossfire. It's as silly as a conservative trying to win liberals over to conservatism by acting like a liberal himself...utterly ridiculous. All he gains is everyone's contempt.

Jesus warned us about this in Matthew 16:25.

"For whosoever will save his life shall lose it: and whosoever will lose his life for my sake shall find it. For what is a man profited, if he shall gain the whole world, and lose his own soul...?" (Matthew 16:25)

Our Lord made it very clear that living carnally would cost us spiritually. His use of the word "life" in Matthew 16:25 refers not only to our physical existence in general but also to the elements that make up that physical existence like one's own flesh, emotions, ego, money, possessions, home, family, career AND YES, even one's own ministry. Matthew 16:25 applies not just to those of us sitting in the pews, but also to those of us standing in the pulpits. Unfortunately, many of today's pulpit standers have erroneously concluded that "protecting their ministry" is the first order of business, as if God relied on that pastor for HIS survival and protection rather than the pastor relying on God for his. My question for these misguided shepherds is this: If it is YOUR job to protect your ministry then whose job is it to carry out that ministry while you're busy protecting it...o ye of little faith"?

If pastor Falwell needed someone to blame for our country's moral decline and current catastrophes he should have started his search a little closer to home and pointed his fearless finger at today's salt-free saints and the reverends of relativism that make up the postmodernist church of political correctness. What is offered in our multi-million dollar sensory-driven sanctuaries is no more lasting or satisfying than a Saturday matinee. But, because today's seeker-sensitive Christians see no difference in evangelism and entertainment they're convinced that whatever's showing down at the church is "AWESOME" as long as the name Jesus appears somewhere in the credits. Today's pop church requires RELAT-ivism to effectively RELATE to the world and make itself "hip" enough to form the kind of RELATIONSHIPS that will bring in the cash, crowds, celebrities and charisma necessary to sustain a state-of-the-art experience they call "worship".

And so now, even in church, we are tempted to serve the creation rather than the Creator. If we try to serve both by straddling that fence, then we, like Pastor Falwell, will offend both and the world will cheer as they watch us go down in flames.

"No man can serve two masters: for either he will hate the one, and love the other; or else he will hold to the one, and despise the other. Ye cannot serve God and mammon." (Matthew 6:24)[37]

"Testimonies of Young People and Christian Rock"

"By their fruits ye shall know them . . ."

"I was following the Lord wholeheartedly until we switched churches and I was invited to the new youth group. I had a conviction against rock music, but as I was surrounded by it, my beliefs were corrupted. This music eventually led to rebellion and

moral failures. The Lord has gained victory in my life now, but the music still brings on rebellion if I listen to it. Please get rid of this music and play melodious, harmonious music!"
—A Fifteen-Year-Old Student From Pennsylvania

"'Christian rock' had made me a shallow, rebellious young Christian. It made it easy for me to get into regular rock music. When I finally submitted to God and got the rock music out of my life, I was able to see the double standard that is lived out by 'Christian rock' musicians.

" 'Christian rock' does not praise God and it is worse than regular rock because I think it is hypocritical. Rock is wrong and addictive and has contributed to my moral failure. I praise God for His help in releasing me from it."
—An Eighteen-Year-Old Student From Indiana

"About four years ago, a local Christian radio station began broadcasting 'rock' of the 'Christian variety.' At first, I accepted only the light stuff. Within months, I found myself listening to heavier and heavier stuff. I thank God that my parents and I came to an agreement on the music I will listen to. I can see how it has affected the lives of some who at one time were my closest friends. I still enjoy easy classical music, but they are into heavy worldly rock and the lifestyle that goes with it. Just a few weeks ago, God convicted me of what I once considered super-soft, contemporary music. I threw the tape away and thank God for the conviction that brought me to do it."
—A Twenty-Year-Old Student From Kansas

"I began to listen to 'Christian rock' without the blessing of my father. He told me that if I listened to 'Christian rock' it would open the door for Satan. I just laughed, and listened anyway. It totally deadened my Christian growth and led to terrible immorality, rebellion, and rejection of God. It then developed into secular,

hard rock. Now all I can do is go back and pick up the pieces. But I still have a scar in my life that will never be removed."
—A Sixteen-Year-Old Student From Oklahoma

When I got into 'Christian' and secular rock, I went out from under my father's protection. I lost sleep, was rebellious, had a rotten attitude, and made life miserable for my parents. I also had major impure thoughts. I no longer listen to that music, and life is so much more enjoyable and I have much more spiritual victory. Whenever I hear this music, I get uptight and am tempted to get back into it.

Thank God I am not in it anymore."
—A Seventeen-Year-Old Student From Texas

"'Christian rock' has hindered my life because the only difference between 'Christian rock' and secular rock is the words. The beat, rhythm, and the melody are not different; they are the same.

"It does not matter whether I listen to secular or 'Christian rock,' when the songs are over, I feel the same. I feel an emptiness in my soul, a heavy burden. Even 'Christian rock' sometimes makes me feel like going out and getting rowdy or even hurting someone else if they provoke me, and that is against all of God's teachings, and everything God stands for. So get rid of all rock!!!"
—A Twenty-One-Year-Old Student From Michigan

"When I was twelve or thirteen years old, I was given some 'Christian rock' tapes by my parents to listen to because they thought I was getting into secular music. The truth is, I was getting into some bad music. The 'Christian rock' dominated my life for over a year until I could not get the same satisfaction I received the first time I heard it. I went to secular rock music and kept this desire and sin from my parents. I started out on soft music and grew to pop/rock-type music.

"It was not long until my desire grew to 'hard rock' and 'progressive' stuff. I started getting into drinking and going to dance clubs. Minor recreational drugs came in and soon my life was going down the drain.

"One night while drinking, I fell into immorality and my life was devastated. God used this tragedy to turn me around and bring me back to Him. I feel very deeply that if I had not started out in 'Christian rock' I would have been convicted about the bad music I got into. Maybe I would not have messed my life up so much."
—An Eighteen-Year-Old Student From Oklahoma

"'Christian rock' was brought into my life earlier than my peers because of a weakness in my forefathers. I continually desired music that had a strong and fast beat. The music I started with was soft, slow, and contemporary, and it took over my life and I became dependent upon it rather than upon God. I did not realize it, but I was a lukewarm Christian, no matter how many times I sought God at the altar. Eventually, my parents saw the folly of Christian contemporary music and took it out of our home. After it was gone, the music took less precedence in my life, and God gave me the conviction to not listen to evil Christian contemporary music. He made me free in my soul!"
—A Sixteen-Year-Old Student From Illinois

"When I was twelve I began listening to 'Christian rock.' My friends listened to it and I felt pressured to listen to it, too. I became addicted to the beat and slowly progressed until I was into 'heavy metal Christian.' I was talking to a boy in our church about rock music. He told me I listened to the same thing in 'Christian rock.' I decided to listen and find out for myself. The beat was exactly the same, and I quickly was addicted to rock. I have been working on conquering this, but when I hear any 'Christian rock' I immediately feel guilty and stay away from my parents."
—A Fifteen-Year-Old Student From Florida

'Christian rock' at one time really messed up my view of Christianity. I would listen to it and think, 'Look how Christianity is trying to blend in with the world.' . . . I have totally avoided this music and have considered it ungodly and unscriptural!"

"Benny Hinn"

Benny Hinn has taken "faith healing" to a new level and developed this art into a greater "spectator sport" made for television. Most all of his services conclude with some sort of miracle healing- -real or unreal- -which have the "hype" and flavor of a championship game. Mr. Hinn immediately becomes the recipient of all the glory and attention that ultimately belongs to God. This in itself is heresy and hypocrisy of gigantic proportions.

Recently I witnessed a Benny Hinn crusade service where a young lad of Spanish extraction supposedly received his sight. The conversation and details were performed through an interpreter—to add extra drama and mystique to the unfolding of events. In the end, however, this lad was able to see with the help of Benny Hinn as mediator and intercessor.

From my experience the majority of "faith healers" are likened to magicians—both using tricks for the purpose of deception. How, then, can the blind be made to see? Temporary blindness can be caused with eye-drops, and sight can be quickly restored with the aid of other eye solutions. Thus, "once I was blind, but now I see." Keep in mind this ancient proverb: "Believe nothing you hear, and only half of what you see; and never, ever play with bumble bees."

The following newspaper article is reprinted with permission in its entirety:

"Grab the popcorn, get set for sermon"
Velocity Church offers music, video preaching at movie house

Pick up popcorn and a soda at the concession, settle back in a comfy seat and look up at the big screen. What's coming up is not the latest release from Hollywood, it's a video sermon.

Welcome to Velocity Church. No ticket needed and there's even a choice of music: rock 'n' roll or pop country.

Velocity is the area's newest congregation, and it meets at the Short Pump Regal Cinemas. The nondenominational church held its first worship services March 19.

"It's a fun church done just outside the box," said Tim Cole, Velocity's lead minister.

When worshipers arrive in the theater lobby, they can drop off their children and choose a venue. The rock 'n' roll and pop-country music services run simultaneously, Cole said. The church uses six of the movie house's fourteen theaters, two for worship and four for nursery and Sunday-school classes.

"We hope to have three or four options. A more traditional service maybe. We would be open to jazz gospel. Just anything we are able to staff and support that will allow us to attract the most people the most effectively," he said.

Cole and his staff of four want to reach people who don't go to church. The approximately twenty-five minute sermons come from Community Christian Church in Chicago. "We are able to select great preaching from great preachers. We can control the quality of the sermons by only showing the good ones," Cole said.

"And rather than spending twenty or more hours every week in sermon preparation, I can focus more on what our church is doing in the community and ministries," Cole said. "I will MC the services."

Each service has the same sermon. Only the music is different. The two church bodies are connected through what Cole calls gel groups. These are small groups that will meet during the week in homes so worshipers can make spiritual friendships to share their faith journey: "We feel faith is not meant to be done alone," he said.

Every Sunday morning, Velocity's staff will back up a trailer to the theater and unload its sound system, lights and media equipment and turn the theater into a church. They need to vacate the theater before the flicks take over the big screens around noon.

Glen Allen resident Pam Dumke is on the launch team for the new church. "Velocity is totally different from anything anybody has seen here," she said. "I see so many people who aren't affiliated with a church, and they don't have that bond with a church family that is so important for my husband and I."

Velocity is the thirteenth house of worship started in the state by Virginia Vision since 1990. The Virginia group was created by the Fellowship of Independent Christian Churches to start churches around the state.

Velocity means speed with direction, said Cole, who also is Virginia Vision's director. "We believe everybody is on a spiritual journey. We hope to help people accelerate their journey toward God."[38]

"Gimmicks and Gadgets"

From wild side to church: Ex-stripper-turned-preacher evangelizes to sex industry

The phone rang—again—and Heather Veitch answered from her three-bedroom tract home here. It was yet another radio station, this time from Detroit, and the DJ wanted to hear the tale of the stripper turned evangelist.

"I don't try to change their life," she said of the women she seeks out at strip clubs. "I just want them to have a relationship with God." The DJ then throws a curveball: Isn't it a sin to strip? "It is a sin to strip," she answered quickly, "but it's okay to strip for your husband."

Veitch then makes an on-air confession. "I strip for my husband," she said with a wide smile, "and I teach women in my church how to do it, too."

She has been called the pin-up preacher and porn again. On Thursday she was introduced on evangelist Pat Robertson's "The 700 Club" as a "holy hottie."

Veitch describes herself simply as an evangelist, the head of a trio of missionaries and JC's Girls Girls Girls.

Every month, JC's Girls (JC is for Jesus Christ) and a few female volunteer church members visit strip clubs, where they pay for lap dances. While alone with a stripper in a booth, they forgo the dance and share the Gospel.

In January, JC's Girls went to Las Vegas for the AVN Adult Entertainment Expo, regarded as the nation's largest trade show in the porn business, and handed out more than two hundred Bibles wrapped in "Holy Hottie" T-shirts.

Veitch, 31, who was a striper for four years, founded the outreach ministry last March.

A few months later, she and fellow member Lori Albee launched an edgy Web site—www.jcgirls.com—that trades on the sex appeal of JC's Girls to attract visitors. Against a violet background, provocative appeals appear: "If you are a CHRISTIAN...See us in ACTION."

None of this caused much of a stir until the Daily Telegraph in England published a story on the ministry Dec. 5. The phone has not stopped ringing since then.

Veitch has been profiled in newspapers and on radio and has made the rounds of network and cable television.

She has appeared on tabloid TV, but last week's appearance on "The 700 Club" took her straight into Christian homes. Robertson's show drew an average of 863,000 viewers a day during the 2004-05 television season, Nielsen Media Research said.

And the offers keep pouring in: movies, books, reality shows, more documentaries. Veitch sees a higher purpose in all the publicity. "Every time I go on a radio station," she said, "I'm spreading God's message."

Not everyone agrees. "I'm a little offended that she would use the Bible in such a sensuous manner," said the Rev. Ray Turner, pastor of Temple Missionary Baptist Church in San Bernardino. He noted that JC's Girls does not urge strippers to leave the sex industry.

"How can you stay in the industry and have a relationship with God?" he asked. "You can't serve two masters at one time."

Turner, however, did praise her efforts. "I commend her for her zeal and desire to reach the lost for Christ," he said.

The Rev. Matt Brown, founder and pastor of the 1,700-member Sandals Church in Riverside, home of JC's Girls, approved a budget of $50,000 for the ministry in January—up from $10,000 in 2005.

"Some people in our church were concerned that some of their offerings and tithes were paying for lap dances," said Brown, 34.

But Brown says that budget—a large portion of which goes to Veitch's salary-is a "drop in the bucket" compared to the funding of the sex industry. "We're really trying to speak to this industry that has been largely ignored by the evangelical church," he said.

He says some of his church members think it is a waste of time to minister to strippers. But Brown is not willing to write them off, he said, especially given Veitch's conversion.

Raised in Muscoy, Calif., a town of 9,000 people in San Bernardino County, Veitch grew up skinny, poor and sad. "I was the girl from the wrong side of the tracks," she said, recalling how she was teased mercilessly by her peers.

At fourteen, she accepted a ride from a stranger on her way to school and ended up in a hotel room, where he raped her. Veitch didn't report it because she was embarrassed. After that, she says, she became promiscuous. At seventeen, she became pregnant while attending continuation school. The twenty-two year-old father, she said, turned out to be a deadbeat.

Veitch became a stripper in 1995 when she was twenty-one and says she eventually made $1,200 to $2,000 a night. She appeared in four soft-core and fetish films and lived life on the wild side.

By 1999, though, the thrill of fast money, hard drinking and fantasy enabling was gone.

Veitch planned to leave the business before the millennium, and she said she thought the world would end. "I was starting to get nervous that if I died I was going to pay the price for how I lived," she said.[39]

Let not sin therefore reign in your mortal body, that ye should obey it in the lusts thereof; For the wages of sin *is* death. *(Romans 6:12,23a)*

CHAPTER 8

BIG BUSINESS

"The things that will destroy America are prosperity at any price, peace at any price, duty first instead of safety first, the love of soft living, and the get rich theory of life."
—Theodore Roosevelt

Can you remember years ago when life was more simple, churches were smaller; money was still tight but wasn't needed as much because budgets were smaller? The preacher was the only one on the payroll, while the men of the church cut the grass, trimmed the hedges, did the painting, and the ladies did the cleaning and polishing. On Sundays the congregation did the singing with a piano player who often missed a note or two. These were the "good-old days"—simple folks and no "so-called" professionals.

Today, however, the church has a pastor, an assistant or two, a youth director, secretaries, janitors, maintenance and helpers, board of directors, marketing agents, counselors, and whoever else one might find a need for. The "biggies" even have lawyers on the payroll to keep the leadership out of jail. Committees are set-up for everything from social functions to fund-raising. Ministers have forsaken prayer and Bible reading, while becoming "con artists" to raise more and more money. The Bible teaches us to "owe no man any thing" (Romans 13:8). The world and carnal man, however, tells us to borrow—buy now and pay back later. Sad to say the Christian and the church have adopted this worldly concept as well. When borrowing, "one becomes a servant to the lender;" tension and pressure mounts with this indebtedness causing instability and lack of control. Churches engaged in this activity soon lose focus and fail to properly minister to the people.

> *"I want to build a university that will one day have a student enrollment of thirty-five thousand, with a football team that can defeat Notre Dame."*
> —Reverend Falwell

Have you ever wondered why businessmen desire to become chief executive officers (CEO) of companies? Because not only do they gain prestige, they control the cash flow. A few years ago it was reported that Bill Smith, then the CEO of General Motors Corporation, had established satellite companies to do subcontract work in the automotive world. He saw to it that a large percentage of General Motor's work was performed by his companies. This is common practice among business people and most all the CEO's receive kickbacks in one form or another. However, when these kind of confidential agreements flow over into the religious sector of society—tax-free organizations—coercion of this nature becomes illegal. Religious institutions receive and parlay millions of dollars each year, with much of the money going directly or indirectly to the CEO's—the televangelist—and their families. Their influence used for favors, friendship, and profit.

> *"If big churches and religious organizations choose to become big business, then they should be treated as such and taxed accordingly."*
> —G.T. Bigelow

Part I: Jim Bakker's PTL Network

Prior to his conviction of bilking nearly $58 million from 120,000 followers, Jim Bakker planned and built Heritage USA, a theme park in Fort Mill, South Carolina. This retreat was a 2,300 acre project consisting of: a Pentecostal church, an extravagant five hundred room hotel, dozens of boutiques, a shopping mall, and amphitheaters with stages, swimming pools, and golf courses. Heritage USA ranked second only to Disneyland and Disney World. However, the one small problem was that although the money had been donated for it, the project was never completed. The PTL Network, second behind Pat Robertson's CBN in Christian cable in Virginia Beach, Virginia, brought in excess of $100 million annually.

Huge salaries, bonuses, and a lavish lifestyle depleted most of the donations. The Charlotte Observer reported that Jim and Tammy Bakker and other top executives received "horrendous and indefensible" salaries as well as other compensation. Prior to resigning Tammy Faye Bakker received nearly $1.6 million with an additional 640,000-dollar bonus.[40]

Jim Bakker's top assistant, Richard Dortch, received $350,000 a year, while his executive secretary received $360,000. Diamonds and other jewelry, luxury cars, expensive clothes, and exotic vacations amounted to another $one million on a yearly basis. Former Vice President George Bush's press secretary until 1984, Peter B. Teeley, received $120,000 in consulting fees—the organization's Washington "liaison," according to the Washington Post.[41] Executive type health coverage with no deductibles paid for Tammy Faye's breast enlargement and Jim's face lift—to retain his boyish look. Twenty-one other top officials received this same coverage paid for by donations to the ministry. And there is strong support among former Bakker associates that he has several million in a Swiss bank account.

Part II: Old-Time Gospel Hour

The Old-Time Gospel Hour filed suit in July 1980, contending that the state's tax laws and constitution exempt it from paying taxes. City attorneys for Lynchburg said the Gospel Hour, the fund-raisers, and financial managers for Reverend Falwell's organizations, do not meet requirements for a religious organization.

Approximately thirty-five of the fifty-five parcels owned by the Gospel Hour produced income. Some of the leases in the Gospel Hour's building include a "high class" beer joint, a grocery store, and a correctional house. A great combination, to say the least, for old-time sinful preaching.

By the way, guess who won the bout in the courts? That's right! Lynchburg forgave the church, Old-Time Gospel Hour, and affiliated ministries for failing to pay past taxes, and also gave it increased tax breaks for the future because of local business pressures.

Ever since the early 1970's the Securities and Exchange Commission (SEC) has been, at times, investigating the Thomas Road Baptist Church and its ministries for selling securities and floating bonds. As recent as January, 1995, Daniel Reber and Jimmy Thomas, supporters of Liberty University, purchased bonds from bondholders at discount prices totaling close to $40 million. These creditors accepted approximately one-eighth of the face value of their investment, for fear of not receiving any payment. By God's law, however, the church and university still owe these people money.

> *"Owe no man any thing, but to love one another: for he that loveth another hath fulfilled the law."*
> —Romans 13:8

Part III: Rev. Moon's Moonies

The Reverend Sun Myung Moon—a Korean-born evangelist who says he is the next messiah—heads the cultist Unification Church. Moon enjoys having thousands of dedicated followers who collect him millions of dollars each year by standing in front of department stores and supermarkets all across America. They claim to give the donations to starving children and for the spread of the gospel; however, the greatest portion of this money is ultimately squandered on Sun Moon's selfish ambitions.

In recent years Reverend Moon has sought political power in the United States at the grass-roots level. Since 1982 Moon has financed *The Washington Times*, a conservative newspaper in the nation's capital. Moon has said his long-term objective is formation of a 'Christian political party' that would encompass all religious sects. For the moment he has become active, through a labyrinth of corporations, in funding two seemingly disparate interests: conservative organizations, particularly the religious right, and civil-rights activists.[42]

Moon's Unification Church also supported the American Freedom Coalition (AFC), a right-wing group that strongly supports Nicaraguan contras. Also, a supporter of this group is Pat Robertson's CBN—who enjoys a close alliance with former Lt. Colonel Oliver North and Jerry Falwell.

Then, why do conservative activists choose to close ranks with a cultist leader? Because right-wing fund raising, in recent years, has fallen on hard times—they are in great need of fresh revenue. When it comes down to Christianity or money, then Christians generally choose money the majority of the time.

> *"Be you not unequally yoked together with unbelievers: for what fellowship hath righteousness with unrighteousness? And what communion hath light with darkness? And what concord hath Christ with Belial? Or what part hath he that believeth with an infidel?"*
> —II Corinthians 6:14,15

Part IV: Oral Roberts' Faith City

The City of Faith in Tulsa, Oklahoma, was founded by America's most famed faith healer—Oral Roberts. Inside this compound lies the five thousand student Oral Roberts University and a 294-bed City of Faith hospital. There is a $20 million Healing City dedicated to his "star son" and heir apparent to the empire Richard Roberts. The ministries air two programs—"Expect a Miracle" and "Richard Roberts Live"—on Christian Broadcasting Network, Trinity Broadcasting Network, and Black Entertainment Television. The annual budget exceeds $130 million with the large majority coming from donations.

Roberts drives a Mercedes—one of several—lives in a home in Tulsa worth several million and owned by Oral Roberts University, owns a home of equal or greater value in Rancho Mirage, California, and uses for entertainment an exclusive and lavish home in Beverly Hills owned by his organization. Sources at the Roberts' headquarters in Tulsa confirmed the existence of the property, but would not put a tag on it.

Remember, it was Roberts who was widely criticized for saying God told him he would die unless his fund-raising goal of $8 million was reached in three months. He drew international attention for spending a ten day vigil in his prayer tower at Oral Roberts University. When the money finally came in, Roberts later said that the Lord also told him to ask for the same amount every year.

"Jesus said unto him, It is written again, Thou shalt not tempt the Lord thy God."
—Matthew 4:7

Misappropriation of Funds

"I hope I shall possess firmness and virtue enough to maintain what I consider the most enviable of all titles, the character of an honest man."
—George Washington

Crystal Cathedral

Pastor Robert Schuller is a bland-looking theatrical performer who presides over the $20 million Crystal Cathedral in Garden Grove, California—paid for by donations from viewers. The weekly "Hour of Power" program reaches 2.5 million people on an annual budget of about $45 million and $6 million on non-TV operations. The 10,000-member church is associated with the mainline Reformed Church in America—it promotes "hyperoptimism."

Several years ago the glittery Crystal Cathedral was ordered by the state of California to pay $473,000 in back taxes—money from ticket sales to concerts that made a profit for Schuller and his ministries. These concerts featured such names as: the Fifth Dimension, Tony Bennett, and Lawrence Welk. Mr. Schuller delivered the check to the state personally.

These profits—several million dollars—gained from secular enterprises were used to give Schuller and his top ranking executives additional fringe benefits—bonuses, housing, vacations, and miscellaneous expenses. This "God loves you, and so do I" religion that Schuller preaches, is aimed at giving man, not God, the credit for thinking positively. This "hyperoptimism" is people pleasing to the point of pernicity.

Robert Tilton

One of the biggest phonies to be aired on television in recent years is Reverend Robert Tilton—who is everything but reverent. Tilton, headquartered out of Dallas, Texas, portrayed himself as a charismatic fanatic—a modern-day demagogue. He would make false promises—in the name of God—to TV listeners who sent in faith promise pledges. The more money a person sent in to the ministry would be compensated by God to you in the form of more abundant monetary blessings. The Tilton Ministries was taking in over $4 million each month when the news media uncovered his little scam.

Tilton feigned spiritual intercession through his "unknown tongue" babblings and eye-blinking techniques from his prayer room within the studios. He was often pictured praying over cards and letters sent in by faithful viewers seeking divine help promised by Tilton. The news discovered that the cards and letters were in reality discarded into a dumpster behind the studios, while the checks were deposited and redirected to personal use immediately. The donations were used for such luxuries as: a $2 million yacht, expensive homes and real estate, fat bank accounts, and international travel. Tilton's followers were left with broken promises and a debt to pay.

It would seem that the directive to Tilton's staff to throw away the prayer requests was the catalyst to his "downfall," but he is by no means gone from the scene—only perhaps a bit less ostentatious. Tilton is still raking it in through his vast television audience and harvesting millions from his mailing list and programs on Black Entertainment Television.

Of course questions from the media poured in seeking an explanation about the mail scandal. Two of his closest associates, James Ferris and Dan Moroso refused to divulge any information about their 'boss.' But then, Tilton is president of Liberator Productions, a nonprofit in Miami and Moroso is vice president.

One of several lawsuits filed against Tilton amounted to $1.5 million was reversed on appeal. Apparently, Tilton's viewers were taken in by his ability to make them feel good about themselves. He gives them hope and in return, they give him generous donations. In other words, the guy ranks in the top fifth percentile of scam artists!

> *"There is a conspiracy of her prophets in the midst thereof, like a roaring lion ravening the prey: they have devoured souls; they have taken the treasure and precious things."*
> —Ezekiel 22:25

Catholic Capers

In 1993 we read in the newspapers about the Italian police cracking down and arresting members of the Mafia in Rome and Sicily. Why after all these years in power were these so-called "untouchables" finally being brought to justice? The chief reason is that the Vatican stopped supporting the Mafia—a protection agency for the ecclesiastical providence in Rome, Italy. Yes, money donated by Catholics—largely from the archdiocese in the United States—helped fund these notorious "thugs" to protect Vatican City.

How about the war in Northern Ireland that has raged for three decades? The Irish Republican Army (IRA), British troops, and the Roman Catholics have been at the throats of one another for years. Again money from the catholic dioceses has funded the Royal Ulster Constabulary, the provincial police force, with millions of dollars over the years for protection of Irish Catholics.

The latest incident involving money and the shuffling of power has occurred in Haiti. What was the real force behind restoring President Jean-Bertrand Aristide back to power? Again it was pressure and dollars from the U.S. archdiocese. President Aristide is a catholic priest who now dabbles in voodoo. In fact a voodoo festival is celebrated in Haiti the last week of March. As President, a position of power and influence, Aristide can greatly advance the catholic cause in a country like Haiti as it has been advanced in so many others "third world countries."

United Way

William Aramony, former president of the nation's largest and most visible charity, squandered over $650,000 to maintain a lavish lifestyle and romance young women. Aramony served twenty-two years as president of United Way, a charity which raises $3.5 billion annually. Friends say he is a back-slapping charismatic of catholic background and a born salesman.

Aramony established spin-off companies with charitable monies which gave one former girlfriend $80,000 in illicit payments. His staff and United Way directors also got a piece of the action for not blowing the whistle as they watched Bill Aramony womanize and misuse the company bank accounts. The ethical climate of an organization generally starts at the top and flows downhill.

> *"Let not sin therefore reign in your mortal body,*
> *that you should obey it in the lusts thereof."*
> —Romans 6:12

Ex-charity exec lived lavishly

Prosecutors: United Way funds squandered on luxuries

The former head of the nation's best-known charity spent hundreds of thousands of the charity's dollars to maintain a lavish lifestyle and romance young women, federal prosecutors said Monday.

William Aramony and two former United Way of America associates stole more than $1 million to pay for chauffeur-driven gambling sprees and an elegant New York City apartment for Aramony's seventeen year-old girlfriend, Assistant U.S. Attorney Randy Bellows said at the start of Aramony's fraud trial. "The simple truth of this case is how these three men at the pinnacle of their professions abused their positions of trust in order to enrich themselves," Bellows said.

Aramony, 67, was indicted in September on fifty-three felony counts of fraud, conspiracy and money laundering. He served twenty-two years as president of the organization that oversees about 2,800 local United Way chapters nationwide.

Aramony has pleaded innocent. Prosecutors say that under federal sentencing guidelines, he would probably be sentenced to about six years if convicted on all the charges.

His attorney, William Moffitt, told a U.S. District Court jury of eight women and four men that Aramony was a brilliant money-raiser who dedicated his life to the United Way. In his final year, the charity raised about $3.5 billion, Moffitt said.

Moffitt said United Way's board of directors—including some of the heads of the nation's largest corporations—knew about and approved many of Aramony's spending practices. The board turned on Aramony after news accounts in 1992 publicly detailed the expenditures, he said.

"Then a blissful ignorance of what was going on at the United Way descended from the corporate mists," Moffitt said.[43]

AMI Securities

The AMI Investment Corporation of Amarillo, Texas, supposedly a Christian organization, filched tens of thousands of investors into believing they were buying no-risk investments. These investors bought church bonds of already troubled institutions and other not-for-profit organizations.

AMI brokers told investors "that the banks in Texas were falling apart, and they were doing the work of the Lord to take their money out of banks and put it into church bonds," said Henry Seals, the court-appointed trustee for the Church and Institutional Facilities Development Corporation, an AMI subsidiary that entered bankruptcy proceedings in October 1990.[44]

AMI Securities—working in behalf of Christians—issued $250 million in bonds on behalf of American churches with only $3.5 million of insurance to cover losses. The S.E.C. contended that besides selling unsecured bonds, AMI directors and former president, Willard E. May, pocketed commissions and other processing fees. And one of the largest clients of AMI was Jerry Falwell's Old-Time Gospel Hour—friend of Willard May. Mr. May also gave the ministry an additional $3 million—money due other investors for mature bonds—to build a football stadium for Chancellor Falwell's Liberty University. Thus, investors have never been fully reimbursed.

"Owe no man anything, but to love one another."
—Romans 13:8

Tele-Evangelist Lifestyles: Halls of Shame

"Christianity began as a personal relationship with Jesus Christ. When it went to Athens, it became a philosophy. When it went to Rome, it became an organization. When it went to Europe, it became a culture. When it came to America, it became a business."
—In Plain Site

L. Ron Hubbard, founder of Scientology, once said "Writing for a penny a word is ridiculous. If a man really wanted to make a million dollars, the best way would be to start his own religion." While our modern day evangelists have not started their own religion, they have unquestionably improved on Hubbard's idea. Capitalizing on Christianity has proved to be far more lucrative than starting a new religion. Some examples of this fact are compiled below.

Jim and Tammy Bakker:

The Bakkers bought mansions and luxury cars and the doghouse was air-conditioned.[45] "Jim Bakker, who was convicted of wire fraud and served five years in prison, said he plans to start another TV ministry, this time in Branson, Missouri."[46]

Juanita Bynum:

The "million-dollar" wedding of Dr. Juanita Bynum, well-known evangelist and author of the best-selling Matters of the Heart, to Bishop Thomas W. Weeks III featured a wedding party of eighty, all friends and family, 1,000 guests, a twelve-piece orchestra, and a 7.76-carat diamond ring. The black-tie wedding cost "more than a million," the bride said, and included flowers flown in from around the world. "My dress," she says, "took nine months to make. All of the crystals (Swarovski) on the gown were hand-sewn. The headpiece was sterling silver, hand-designed.[47]

The Crystal Cathedral:

"In September of 1959, ground-breaking ceremonies were held at the location of the present church property in Garden Grove, California. The Crystal Cathedral was completed in 1980, from which Schuller now tapes his weekly service and later broadcasts on his weekly "Hour of Power" television show (begun in 1970). This cathedral is a vast golden edifice with 10,000 windows, huge video screens, and a ten foot tall angel hovering from the roof on a rope of gold. He has built up a congregation of over 9,500 members in a church that cost over $20 million.

The "Tower of Power" television ministry makes more than $50 million a year and is beamed to about twenty million viewers in more than 180 countries. Schuller claims to receive between thirty and forty thousand letters a week and has a mailing list of over one million people. He has authored more than twenty-five books, several of them national best sellers."

Made almost entirely of glass (and a spider web framework of white steel), the star-shaped "cathedral" is something to behold: over four hundred feet long and two hundred feet across, rising some twelve stories above the ground, with an angular, mirror-like exterior, its transparent, sun-lit interior features a giant television screen, and an altar of rich marble (bearing a natural image that some think resembles Christ on the cross). The cathedral's pipe organ (with sixteen thousand pipes, it's among the five largest pipe organs in the world), the one hundred plus voices of the Hour of Power Choir, or the electric fountain/stream that runs down the middle of the central aisle. The church seats almost three thousand worshipers for Sunday services. But giant, sliding glass doors on the side of the church allow even more worshipers to watch the services from their cars in the parking lot.

Boasting over twelve thousand panes of glass, and a sparkling, contemporary bell tower, the "cathedral" is an Orange County landmark visible for miles around. The new glass tower was added in 1990, and is a stunning edifice in its own right; at the tower's base you will find a tiny, dome-shaped chapel housing an uncommon, cross-shaped crystal. Instead the usual wooden church pews, the "cathedral" offers soft, theatre-style, individual seats (each bearing a small plaque with the name of a donor). During Sunday services, the church offers a nursery and childcare services.[48]

The Crouch's Homes:

Televangelists Jan and Paul Crouch of the Costa Mesa-based Trinity Broadcasting Network have purchased a Newport Beach house for close to $5 million, Orange County Realtors say. The home was described as "a palatial estate with ocean and city views." The Crouches had been living in a smaller house in the same neighborhood. The house they bought has six bedrooms, nine bathrooms, a billiard room, a climate-controlled wine cellar, a sweeping staircase and a crystal chandelier. The three-story, nearly 9,500-square-foot house, which has an elevator, also has a six-car garage, a tennis court and a pool with a fountain. The house is on slightly more than an acre. Jan Crouch wanted a bigger yard for her dogs, sources said.[49]

One of the Crouch estates is TBN's ranch in Colleyville, TX, just minutes away from the Dallas/Fort Worth International Airport. The 80-plus acre ranch is located between the city limits of Colleyville and Southlake—two of the wealthiest cities in Texas. The ranch, which contains eight houses and horse stables, is estimated to be worth about $10 million. "Hellooooo Woorld!" yells Paul, who has seen much of it in the past twenty-five years. He gets around nowadays in a Canadair Challenger 600 executive jet worth about $13 million.[50]

Wealth Report:

The Crouches and their son Paul Jr. said they earned a total of $855,000 in 2005. Trinity Broadcasting Network's annual earnings reportedly is in excess of $100 million annually. The Crouches' $10 million ranch outside Dallas is accessorized with two Land Rovers. Recently, the couple also purchased a $5 million oceanfront estate in California.

Creflo Dollar:

The ministry's income is unavailable, but newspaper accounts say the ministry paid $18 million in cash for his new 8,000-seat World Changers Church International on the southern edge of Atlanta. He flies to speaking engagements across the nation and Europe in a $5 million private jet and drives a black Rolls-Royce. Dollar's ministry became a focus of a court case involving boxer Evander Holyfield in 1999. The lawyer for Holyfield's ex-wife estimated that the fighter gave Dollar's ministry $7 million. Dollar refused to testify in the case.[51]

The Atlanta Journal-Constitution[52] says this,

> The Rev. Creflo Dollar Jr. has unabashedly embraced his name by building a religious empire on the message that his brand of piety leads to prosperity. He drives a black Rolls-Royce, flies to speaking

engagements across the nation and Europe in a $5 million private jet and lives in a $1 million home behind iron gates in an upscale Atlanta neighborhood. The World Changers campus sits on a slight hill...Inside the church is a lobby befitting a five-star hotel. Chairs are scattered about on baby blue carpet thick enough to muffle the sound of the stadium-size crowd arriving for a Sunday service...There are no visible traditional Christian symbols—no cross, no image of Jesus, no stained-glass windows...Dollar lives in a $1 million home owned by the church in the Guilford Forest subdivision in southwest Atlanta. World Changers purchased another $1 million home on twenty-seven acres in Fayette County in December. The church has amassed a fortune in real estate, mostly in College Park...As World Changers grew, so did Dollar's emphasis on prosperity. Dollar has no degree in theology. Much of his prosperity message, according to church and his family members, are based on the teachings of friend and spiritual mentor Kenneth Copeland...And a frequent criticism—that the church refuses to help non[-]tithers—isn't true either, Lett said. Tithers simply "have priority," she said. People are not allowed to touch Dollar during services, she said, simply because "the anointing is flowing at that point." She said the church purchased a Rolls-Royce for Dollar's use because "he deserves the best."

InPlainSite.org Note—The word *Anointing* has become arguably the most overused, overworked, misunderstood, misinterpreted term in the Pentecostal and Charismatic arenas.[53]

Rev. James Eugene Ewing:

The Rev. James Eugene Ewing built a direct-mail empire from his mansion in Los Angeles that brings millions of dollars flowing into a Tulsa post office box. The approach reaped Ewing and his organization more than $100 million since 1993, including $26 million in 1999, the last year Saint Matthew's made its tax records public. And while much of the money is spent on postage and salaries, Ewing's company receives nonprofit status and pays no federal taxes.

Ewing's computerized mailing operation, Saint Matthew's Churches, mails more than one million letters per month, many to poor, uneducated people, while Ewing lives in a mansion and drives luxury cars.

The letters contain an alluring promise of "seed faith": send Saint Matthew's your money and God will reward you with cash, a cure to your illness, a new home and other blessings. They often contain items such as prayer cloths, a "Jesus eyes handkerchief," golden coins, communion wafers and "sackcloth billfolds." Recipients are often warned to open the letters in private and not discuss them with others.

Though Ewing claims it is a church, Saint Matthew's Church, once called St. Matthew Publishing Inc., has no address other than a Tulsa post office box. It has two listed phone numbers in Tulsa and both are answered by a recorded religious message.

"He capitalizes on the isolation of the loneliest and poorest members of our society, promising them magical answers to their fears and needs if only they will demonstrate their faith by sending him money," Anthony said.

"He is, quite literally, the father of the modern-day 'seed-faith' concept that fuels the multibillion-dollar Christian industry known as the 'health-and-wealth gospel.' "The only ones becoming rich are the men like Ewing." (Ole Anthony is founder of the Trinity Foundation, a nonprofit religious watchdog group). Ewing's flair for effective, dramatic direct-mail appeals won him jobs writing for evangelists including Tilton, Rex Humbard and "Rev. Ike." In many cases, the letters are identical but contain different signatures.

The Trinity Foundation, which obtained copies of the identical letters, has dubbed Ewing "God's Ghostwriter."

"We had nine different televangelists essentially sending out the same letter," Anthony said. "He (Ewing) makes most of his money by selling these packages to televangelists." Anthony said one Ewing letter, written for Humbard, brought in $64 for each copy mailed. Another mailing by Humbard contains a "sackcloth billfold" and asks recipients to mail a "seed offering" of $19 to a Boca Raton, Fla., post office box.

A similar letter from Tilton also contained a "sackcloth billfold" but encouraged recipients to return a "seed of faith" of at least $709.00. Some other facts about St. Matthew's Publishing:

- **1997:** St. Matthew Publishing Inc., incorporated at Joyce's Tulsa law office, files documents with the Internal Revenue Service reporting $15.6 million in revenue. Ewing reports receiving $307,187 in salary and benefits while McElrath reports $277,000 in salary and benefits.

- **1999:** St. Matthew Publishing Inc. reports $26.8 million in revenue. Of that, the organization spent $4 million on salaries, $989,140 on legal fees, $817,000 for housing and rent and $649,000 on travel.[54]

In 1968, Ewing, an eighth-grade dropout, doubled Oral Roberts' cash flow almost overnight with another mail campaign, sources say. Roberts rewarded him with an airplane, according to former Roberts aide Wayne Robinson.[55]

John Hagee:

When John and Diana Hagee co-founded GETV some twenty-five years ago, it was a small one-room Sunday-morning-sermon broadcasting program in San Antonio. It has grown into an extravagant studio of more than fifty thousand square feet, broadcasting to over 100 national television stations and eighty-two radio stations across the country.

The SEC 990s for the organization in 2001 reported it netted $12.3 million in donations, $4.8 million in profit sales of books and tapes, and an additional $1.1 million other sources.

Hagee, the president of the nonprofit was paid $540,000 in compensation plus $302,005 in compensation for his position as president of Cornerstone Church. His GETV benefits package was worth $411,561 with a retirement contributions package usually reserved for highly top-paid executives of corporations that the IRS refers to as "rabbi trusts," apparently titled as such because the first beneficiary of such a package was a rabbi.

The John Hagee Rabbi Trust includes a $2.1 million 7,969-acre ranch outside Brackettville, with five lodges, including a "main lodge" and a gun locker. It also includes a manager's house, a smokehouse, a skeet range and three barns.

All totaled his package is worth $842,005 in compensation and $414,485 in benefits. This was one of the highest (if not the highest) for a nonprofit director in the San Antonio area in 2001.

Diana Hagee's was paid $67,907 as vice president of GETV plus $58,813 as the special events director for Cornerstone Church.[56]

Benny Hinn:

William Lobdell, a *Times* staff member, wrote about target-rich environment: the unregulated industry of televangelism is estimated to generate at least $1 billion through its roughly 2,000 electronic preachers, including 80 nationally syndicated television pastors. He told of the founder of the Dallas-based Trinity Foundation, Ole E Anthony, whose operatives struck dumpster pay dirt five years ago in south Florida when they found a travel itinerary for Benny Hinn, the Trinity Broadcasting Network's superstar faith healer who has filled sports arenas with ailing believers seeking miracle cures. Hinn's itinerary included first-class tickets on the Concorde from New York to London ($8,850 each) and reservations for presidential suites at pricey European hotels ($2,200 a night). A news story, including footage of Hinn and his associates boarding the jet, ran on CNN's "Impact." In addition, property records and videos supplied by Trinity investigators led to CNN and Dallas Morning News coverage of another Hinn controversy: fund-raising for a $30-million healing center in Dallas that has yet to be built.

According to a June article in *The Dallas Morning News*, shortly after Hinn announced his move to Texas, he said God had told him to build a "World Healing Center," and Hinn appealed for money. As much as $30 million was collected, but the center was never built. In April 2000, he told Trinity Broadcasting Network's Paul Crouch, "I'm putting all the money we have in the ministry to get out there and preach. The day (to build the healing center) will come. I'm in no hurry; neither is God."

Also about April 2000, Hinn's ministry began building a 58,000 square-foot office building in Irving. A few months after that, in August 2000, a holding company that is a subsidiary of Hinn's ministry began building a "parsonage"—a $3 million, 7,200-square foot oceanfront home—in Dana Point, Calif.

"Nor has Hinn publicly acknowledged his salary, though he told CNN in 1997 that his yearly income including book royalties was somewhere between $500,000 and $1 million. A spokesman has said Hinn generates about $60 million a year in donations."[57]

However in a report dated 07/06/2005 the Denton Record Chronicle says this:

> "According to documents provided to the newspaper by a watchdog group, the inquiry into the ministry began a year ago and the IRS has asked for dozens of detailed answers. The Trinity Foundation has investigated Hinn for more than a decade. Hinn ministry responses to IRS questions and a purported salary list for ministry officials are among documents that Trinity members said they salvaged from trash bins outside Hinn-related offices. The salary document lists Hinn as CEO and his annual earnings as $1.325 million."[58]

"Since February of 2001, the Hinn Web site has been soliciting donations for a new orphanage to be built in this little town outside Mexico City saying it would be finished "soon." But when we checked in Mexico, more than a year-and-a-half later, we could find no sign of any construction. But the Hinn web site kept promising that construction would be finished in, "a few short months." That was news to the local official in charge of construction in the town, who told us the Hinn ministry hadn't even been issued a building permit yet. What we did find, however, was this sign—curiously not in Spanish, but English—attached to a house the ministry called it's 'temporary orphanage,' which appeared to be empty. The Hinn Web site continued to solicit donations".[59]

"He lives with his wife and three children in a multimillion-dollar oceanfront mansion near the Ritz-Carlton hotel in Dana Point...In an attempt to clear up his image, Hinn suggests meeting a Times reporter at the Four Seasons hotel in Newport Beach.

Accompanied by bodyguards, Hinn arrives in his new Mercedes-Benz G500, an SUV that retails for about $80,000. He is dressed casually in black, from designer sunglasses to leather jacket to shoes...Hinn fiddles with his cell phone, which sports a Mercedes logo. First, Hinn declines to divulge his salary. (He told CNN in 1997 that he earns between $500,000 and $1 million annually, including book royalties.) "Look, any amount I make, somebody's going to be mad," he says...Hinn does reveal that the $89 million taken in by his church in 2002 is a record for his Grapevine, Texas-based ministry, which has experienced double-digit growth during the past three years through direct-mail requests, viewer donations and offerings taken at the Miracle Crusades. By comparison, the Billy Graham Evangelistic Assn. had revenues of $96.6 million in 2001, the last year available.

Many of Hinn's financial practices go against those set forth by the Evangelical Council for Financial Accountability, an organization that gained popularity after the televangelist scandals of the 1980s as Christian groups sought legitimacy in the eyes of donors. The council's standards include maintaining an independent board of directors with at least five members and allowing the public to view its finances."[60]

Revelations from the Benny Hinn program also include:

- Hinn's salary is somewhere between half a million and a million dollars per year. He also gets royalties from the sales of his books;
- Personal perks for Hinn, family and his entourage include a $10 million seaside mansion; a private jet with annual operating costs of about $1.5 million; a Mercedes SUV and convertible, each valued at about $80,000;

- What the church termed "layovers" between crusades included hotel bills ranging from $900 per night to royal suites that cost almost $3,000 for one night's stay. Layover locations included Hawaii, Cancun, London, Milan and other exotic locations.
- Beverly Hills shopping sprees;
- Receipts showing Hinn's daughter receiving $1,300 in petty cash; her boyfriend getting $2,550 for babysitting; $23,000 in cash dispersed to Hinn and his wife; and, $25,000 in cash for expenses for a crusade—thirty minutes away from Hinn's home;
- Hinn continues to espouse the theologically-suspect self-serving Word-of-Faith or "prosperity" gospel. Jesus and his followers never amassed personal wealth through their ministry and instead lived a clearly sacrificial life. Hinn would be wise to follow this example and encourage his followers to do likewise as this would lead to much greater spiritual prosperity, the value of which far exceeds anything material;
- Hinn employs two primary methods to manipulate those that watch him—promising healings to those afflicted with chronic or terminal illnesses, and claiming that donations are "seeds" being planted by the donor that will result in the gift giver enjoying financial blessings;
- Television producer Nathan Daniel, a former BHM employee who was hired to improve the public image, instead reported to NBC, "There was never one complete record that would suit the criteria for documented miracle healing."[61]

Rodney Howard-Browne:

He and his wife, Adonica, oversee his $16 million church, which they founded in 1996. The couple lives in a six-bedroom, four-bath lakefront home on Cory Lake in northwest Tampa. The home includes a dock, spa, pool and gazebo.[62]

T.D. Jakes:

"Jakes, who drives a Mercedes, has moved with his wife and their five children to a luxurious seven-bedroom home with swimming pool in the White Rock Lake area of Dallas.

"Flanked by a row of elegant cedars and surrounded by a tall iron gate, the $2.6 million pink brick house with fluted cream columns and a four-car garage is imposing even in this affluent neighborhood. Next door is the former mansion of oil tycoon H.L. Hunt, once known as the richest man in the world. The Hunt house has been undergoing repairs, and its lawn has withered to beige. These days it almost pales in comparison with its neighbor."[63]

'I do think we need some Christians who are in first class as well as coach,' Jakes said."[64]

The Dallas Observer magazine reports:

"His conferences draw tens of thousands. His television show, broadcast on both the Trinity Broadcasting Network and Black Entertainment Television, reaches hundreds of thousands. He has spawned his own industry, T.D. Jakes Ministries, which sells his books—ten in all, with five best-sellers—and videotapes, the income from which allowed him to spend nearly $1 million last year on a residence in his hometown of Charleston, West Virginia. He says he is not embarrassed by this, even though his extravagant lifestyle has caused controversy in his hometown that will likely follow him to Dallas. His suits are tailored. He drives a brand new Mercedes. Both he and his wife Serita are routinely decked out in stunning jewelry. His West Virginia residence—two homes side by side—includes an indoor swimming pool and a bowling alley. These homes particularly caused the ire of the local folks. One paper wrote at length about the purchase and made much of their unusual features. A columnist dubbed Jakes 'a huckster.' "[65]

James MacDonald:

"The former U.S. Senator Peter Fitzgerald has sold his house in Inverness, severing his lifelong ties with that northwest suburb...Fitzgerald says that when he and his wife decided to sell the house last year, they did not state an asking price. Instead, their agent, Sheila Morgan of ReMax Unlimited Northwest, showed the property to five prospective buyers. James MacDonald, who is the senior pastor of Harvest Bible Chapel in Rolling Meadows and who also delivers a weekly sermon on a Christian radio broadcast, offered $1.9 million—"My minimum," says Fitzgerald—and the deal closed this past October. "It's a very exciting house," says the Rev. MacDonald, 'and it's even better in the backyard.'"[66]

Joyce Meyer—Ministry Headquarters:

The ministry's headquarters is a three-story jewel of red brick and emerald-color glass that, from the outside, has the look and feel of a luxury resort hotel. Built two years ago for $20 million, the building and grounds are postcard perfect, from manicured flower beds and walkways to a five-story lighted cross.

The driveway to the office complex is lined on both sides with the flags of dozens of nations reached by the ministry. A large bronze sculpture of the Earth sits atop an open Bible near the parking lot. Just outside the main entrance, a sculpture of an American eagle landing on a tree branch stands near a man-made waterfall. A message in gold letters greets employees and visitors over the front entryway: "Look what the Lord Has Done."

The building is decorated with religious paintings and sculptures, and quality furniture. Much of it, Meyer says, she selected herself.

A Jefferson County assessor's list offers a glimpse into the value of many of the items: a $19,000 pair of Dresden vases, six French crystal vases bought for $18,500, an $8,000 Dresden porcelain depicting the Nativity, two $5,800 curio cabinets, a $5,700 porcelain of the Crucifixion, a pair of German porcelain vases bought for $5,200.

The decor includes a $30,000 malachite round table, a $23,000 marble-topped antique commode, a $14,000 custom office bookcase, a $7,000 Stations of the Cross in Dresden porcelain, a $6,300 eagle sculpture on a pedestal, another eagle made of silver bought for $5,000, and numerous paintings purchased for $1,000 to $4,000 each.

Inside Meyer's private office suite sit a conference table and eighteen chairs bought for $49,000. The woodwork in the offices of Meyer and her husband cost the ministry $44,000.

In all, assessor's records of the ministry's personal property show that nearly $5.7 million worth of furniture, artwork, glassware, and the latest equipment and machinery fill the 158,000-square-foot building.

As of this summer, the ministry also owned a fleet of vehicles with an estimated value of $440,000. The Jefferson County assessor has been trying to get the complex and its contents added to the tax rolls but have failed.

Stylish sports cars and a plane

Meyer drives the ministry's 2002 Lexus SC sports car with a retractable top, valued at $53,000. Her son Dan, 25, drives the ministry's 2001 Lexus sedan, with a value of $46,000. Meyer's husband drives his Mercedes-Benz S55 AMG sedan. "My husband just likes cars," Meyer said.

The Meyers keep the ministry's Canadair CL-600 Challenger jet, which Joyce Meyer says is worth $10 million, at Spirit of St. Louis Airport in Chesterfield. The ministry employs two full-time pilots to fly the Meyers to conferences around the world.

Meyer calls the plane a "lifesaver" for her and her family. "It enabled us, at our age, to travel literally all over the world and preach the gospel" with better security than that offered on commercial flights, she said.

Security is important to Meyer, who says she has received death threats. She has a division of the ministry dedicated to her safety. Her officers wear pistols; they guard the headquarters' front gate, keeping out anyone but employees and invited guests. The ministry bought a $145,000 house where the security chief lives rent-free to keep him close to the ministry's headquarters.

The family compound

The ministry has also bought homes for other key employees. Since 1999, the ministry has spent at least $4 million on five homes for Meyer and her four children near Interstate 270 and Gravois Road, St. Louis County records show.

Meyer's house, the largest of the five, is a ten thousand square-foot Cape Cod style estate home with a guest house and a garage that can be independently heated and cooled and can hold up to eight cars. The three-acre property has a large fountain, a gazebo, a private putting green, a pool and a pool house where the ministry recently added a $10,000 bathroom.

The ministry pays for utilities, maintenance and landscaping costs at all five homes. It also pays for renovations. The Meyers ordered major rehab work at the ministry's expense right after the ministry bought three of the homes. For example, the ministry bought one home, leveled it and then built a new home on the site to the specifications of Meyer's daughter Sandra and her husband, county records show. Even the property taxes, $15, 629 this year, are paid by the ministry.

Meyer called the homes a "good investment" for the ministry and said the ministry bears the cost of upkeep and maintenance because the family is too busy to take care of such tasks. "It's just too hard to keep up with something like that when you travel as much as we do," Meyer said.

She said that federal tax law allows ministries to buy parsonages for their employees, so the arrangement does not violate any prohibitions against personal benefit. Meyer also said the decision to cluster the families together was a way to build a buffer to better ensure privacy and security.

"We put good people all around us," she said. "Obviously, if I was trying to hide anything or thought I was doing anything wrong, I wouldn't live on the corner of Gravois and 270."

The irrevocable trust

Meyer says she expects the best, from where she lives to how she looks. Much of her clothing is custom-tailored at an upscale West County dress shop. At her conferences, she usually wears flashy jewelry. She sports an impressive diamond ring that she said she got from one of her followers. Meyer has a private hairdresser. And, a few years ago, Meyer told her employees she was getting a face-lift. Not everything is paid directly by the ministry.

Last year, the Meyers bought a $500,000 atrium ranch lakefront home in Porto Cima, a private-quarters club at Lake of the Ozarks. A few weeks later, they bought two watercrafts similar to Jet Skis and a $105,000 Crownline boat painted red, white and blue that they named the Patriot.

In 2000, the Meyers also bought her parents a $130,000 home just a few minutes from where the Meyers live.

The Meyers have put the Mercedes, the lake house, the boat and her parents' home into an irrevocable trust, an arrangement that tax experts say would help protect them from any financial problems at the ministry.

Meyer says she should not have to defend how she spends the ministry's money. "We teach and preach and believe biblically that God wants to bless people who serve Him," Meyer said. "So there's no need for us to apologize for being blessed."

Meyer's "trusted" board

For the most part, Meyer can spend the ministry's money any way she sees fit because her board of directors is handpicked. It consists of Meyer, her husband and all four of her children—all paid workers—as well as six of Meyer's closest friends. (Ministry officials said that daughter Laura Holtzmann has now resigned; state records still list her on the board.) "Our family is a huge help to us," Meyer said. "We couldn't do this if we didn't have somebody we trusted."

Board members Roxane and Paul Schermann are such close friends that for more than a decade they lived in the Meyers' home. The ministry employed both of them as high-level managers and in 2001 bought them a $334,000 home. Roxane Schermann no longer works at the ministry; her husband continues as a paid division manager. The Schermanns bought the house at the same price from the ministry in January. Delanie Trusty, the ministry's certified public accountant, also serves as the ministry board's secretary.

The board decides how the ministry's money is spent. The salaries of Meyer and her family are set by those board members who are not family members and are not employed by the ministry, Meyer's lawyer said. The arrangement meets IRS regulations, the lawyer said.

We certainly wouldn't have enemies and people we don't know" on the board, Meyer said. That wouldn't make any sense. Anybody who has a board is going to have people in favor of you.

Meyer and her ministry refuse to tell how much the ministry pays Meyer, her husband, her children and her children's spouses. "I don't make any more than I'm worth," Meyer said. "We're definitely within IRS guidelines."

Such an overlap between top administrators and board members concerns the IRS because "the opportunity to manipulate and control the organization is easier to accomplish," said Bruce Philipson of St. Paul, Minn., the IRS group manager of tax-exempt organizations for this region.[67]

Mike Murdock:

As president and director of the Mike Murdock Evangelistic Association, Mike Murdock has several luxury vehicles at his disposal. Some belong to him, and some are owned by the ministry. The BMW, worth at least $69,000, was a gift, Murdock says, while the ministry bought the Jaguar. He says he got an idea that allowed him to buy the Cessna Citation 500, worth $300,000 to $500,000. Federal Aviation Administration documents show that the jet belongs to the ministry.

Murdock likes to describe himself as a "Wal-Mart guy." But a $25,000 Rolex adorns his wrist. And he can shoot hoops on the "NBA-style" basketball court at his estate or take notes with a $4,500 fountain pen.

Details of Murdock's lifestyle were pieced together from documents obtained by the Trinity Foundation, a televangelist watchdog group in Dallas; Denton County property-appraisal records; a report of a burglary at his home; interviews; and excerpts from his broadcasts and books. They show a man living a Hollywood lifestyle.

Murdock says he drives a BMW 745, which typically sells for $69,000 to $75,000. He used to prefer driving a Porsche to the ministry. He has had at his disposal a ministry Corvette, Jaguar and Mercedes, Lincoln Continentals and, since August, a corporate jet valued at $300,000 to $500,000.

Murdock lives in a Spanish-style, 3,177-square-foot adobe house that he calls *Hacienda de Paz—or "House of Peace."* He, not the ministry, owns it. Also on the grounds is a 1,660-square-foot building whose use is unclear. The 6.8-acre estate, east of Argyle, was valued at $482,027 by the Denton Central Appraisal District in 2002, documents show.

Few get a good view of the estate. It is protected by a black wrought-iron fence. The gates are monogrammed with two M's—his initials. On the well-kept grounds, a path winds near a tennis court and two of at least four gazebos on the property. At various times, Murdock has had a camel, an antelope, a donkey, ducks, geese, a lion and dogs. Near one edge of his property, he once kept llamas in a paddock. He has also had koi and catfish at the estate. He had twenty-four speakers wired in trees so he could hear gospel music everywhere on the grounds, he said during a 1998 broadcast.

Inside his home, Murdock has had several fish tanks, including a large saltwater aquarium. In the gym, Murdock can work out with his personal trainer. He can relax in front of his home theater or in a Jacuzzi. And he can enjoy the fountains in his pool and living room.

Murdock once kept coin and jewelry collections valued at $125,000. He reported the information to the Denton County Sheriff's Department after a theft. Sheriff's spokesman Kevin Patton said investigators dropped the case because Murdock would not list what had been stolen.

Murdock has a second Rolex watch, besides the $25,000 one he often wears, he said during an appearance Oct. 19 in Grapevine. He didn't state its value.

Murdock has said he was given the watches, expensive suits, several Chevrolet Corvettes, the BMW and a rare Vetta Ventura sports car—one of nineteen made.

From 1993 to 2000, IRS records show his compensation package averaged $241,685 a year, or about 9 percent of the $21,040,299 the ministry took in during that period.[68]

Joel Osteen's Lakewood Church:

"Thirty thousand people endure punishing traffic on the narrow roads leading to Lakewood Church every weekend to hear Pastor Joel Osteen deliver upbeat messages of hope. A youthful-looking forty-two year-old with a ready smile, he reassures the thousands who show up at each of his five weekend services that "God has a great future in store for you." Osteen's best-seller, *Your Best Life Now*, has sold 2.5 million copies since its publication last fall…In his book, Osteen talks about how his wife, Victoria, a striking blonde who dresses fashionably, wanted to buy a fancy house some years ago, before the money rolled in. He thought it wasn't possible. "But Victoria had more faith," he wrote. "She convinced me we could live in an elegant home…and several years later, it did come to pass." Osteen's flourishing Lakewood enterprise brought in $55 million in contributions last year, four times the 1999 amount, church officials say."[69]

Early in 2001, when the city of Houston decided to build a new sports/entertainment complex the powers-that-be placed the Compaq Center (home to the Houston Rockets) on the market. It is extremely unlikely that they dreamed it would be leased by Lakewood church, much less that the church would make a one-time, lump-sum payment of $12 million to the city for the first thirty-year lease period (with an option to renew). This, as it turns out, is only the beginning. After all one has to make the transition from basketball to God, from run of the mill entertainment complex to a place "unlike any other place in the nation"…a $70 million project.

So what kind of place is this one of a kind worship center going to be? According to INJOY Stewardship Services, whom Joel Osteen hired as consultants…"The new complex, which is to be called Lakewood Church Central, will transform the Compaq Center from a sports venue to a 21st century worship center. The main floor, which is now flat (to accommodate basketball and hockey), will be sloped to allow for direct viewing of the platform. Below the main floor, the current locker rooms and administrative offices will become the new Children's Ministry Center-an 85,000-square foot area now being designed by former Disney artists. The exterior of the building will be enhanced with architectural elements that carry the interior design features to the outside. As part of that renovation, new columns will be added to the south and west ends of the building.

The Lakewood Church Central arena will seat over sixteen thousand people yet achieve a sense of intimacy through state-of-the-art sound, lighting and video. The stage area will allow for the Pastor's mobility while providing complete 360-degree visibility to ensure that every seat has a direct view of the pulpit. The stage will be surrounded by three high-definition screens which provide live image support for every service. The new choir loft embraces the worship platform in two curving arcs, with seating for over 250 members.

The Lobby and Food Court, with its dynamic lighting and decorative features, will create a warm atmosphere in which the congregation can gather before and after each service. This new facility will include a bookstore, numerous resource centers, meeting rooms, and information centers conveniently located throughout the lobby area.

Describing his vision for the church's new home, Osteen explains: "We intend to share this great resource and make Lakewood Church Central a gathering point for the entire city of Houston. The ice rink and basketball facilities will remain open for families and city leagues. There will be concerts, sporting events, family conferences, conventions, business workshops, personal growth seminars and much more -and all of these opportunities will bring in people from all walks of life. We're going to touch untold thousands of lives in this place." After it opens in July, he predicts weekend attendance will rocket to 100,000. Says Osteen: "Other churches have not kept up, and they lose people by not changing with the times."

The East Building, a yet-to-be-built four-story complex, will house the International Broadcast and Production Center, the Youth Complex, the main Lakewood Bookstore and the new Grand Entrance. The new broadcast facility will produce Lakewood's weekly television program, the nation's top-rated devotional program as determined by Nielsen Media Research. The Grand Entrance and Lobby will be a spectacular multi-story foyer accessed through towering glass doors. Cascading water features will surround the main stairway and three new escalators leading up to the Worship Center Lobby. An array of new elevators, conveniently located throughout the facility, will aid access to both the Worship Center and the East Building".

Incidentally INJOY's founder John Maxwell was once pastor of a small church in Hillham, Indiana. Studying the "correlation between leadership effectiveness and effective ministry" John founded one business which ultimately led to 'INJOY Stewardship Services'. He resigned his pastorate in 1995 to devote full attention to ISS, seeing "greater potential in the thousands of lives that could be reached through INJOY…" He speaks frequently for several high-profile organizations such as Promise Keepers, Focus on the Family, Sam's Club, Chick-fil-A, Mary Kay, and various Fortune 500 companies.[70]

Oral Roberts:

Roberts' two California homes, partly for security reasons, were not much discussed by the ministry. Oral also remained sensitive about press criticism of his lifestyle. His house in Palm Springs, purchased for $285,000 and financed by a Tulsa bank, was his only privately owned home. In 1982 Oral Roberts University (ORU) endowment funds were used to purchase a $2,400,000 house in a high-security development in Beverly Hills. Considered a potentially profitable investment, the house served as Oral's West Coast office and residence.

Oral's homes in California inevitably kept alive the old questions about his personal wealth and lifestyle. While probably not as probing as the press had been fifteen years earlier, reporters still took a keen interest in Oral's financial affairs. In 1981, the Associated Press published Roberts' personal income figures for the preceding five years—ranging from $70,000 in 1976 to $178,000 in 1978.

Here is a portrait of the real Oral Roberts, the man not too many of his admirers know. He dresses in Brioni suits that cost $500 to $1000; walks in $100 shoes; lives in a $250,000 house in Tulsa and has a million dollar home in Palm Springs; wears diamond rings and solid gold bracelets employees 'airbrush' out of his publicity photos; drives $25,000 automobiles which are replaced every 6 months; flies around the country in a $2 million Fanjet Falcon; has membership, as does his son Richard, in 'the most prestigious and elite country club in Tulsa,' the Southern Hills (the membership fee alone was $18,000 for each, with $130 monthly dues) and in `the ultra-posh Thunderbird Country Club in Rancho Mirage, California' (both father and son joined when memberships were $20,000 each—they are now $25,000); and plays games of financial hanky-panky that have made him and his family members independently wealthy (millionaires) for life.[71]

In addition to his healthy income, derived mostly from book royalties, Oral continued to enjoy generous expense accounts: 'The Roberts's wear expensive clothes and jewelry and travel in a company-owned eight-passenger fanjet.'[72]

Pat Robertson:

Pat Robertson is a wealthy man...an extremely wealthy man. Some estimates put his net worth at 140 million. He lives on the top of a Virginia mountain, in a huge mansion with a private airstrip. He owns the Ice Capades, a small hotel, diamond mines, and until recently, International Family Entertainment, parent company of the Family Channel. How does a televangelist, who is supposedly involved in non-profit work, manage to create such a fortune for himself?[73]

Paula and Randy White:

The Tampa Tribune in an article by Michelle Bearden titled Expensive Walls recently reported: TAMPA—When preachers Randy and Paula White bought the $2.1 million red-brick house on Bayshore Boulevard last month, they were already thinking ahead to November. "We always do a 'Table in the Wilderness' Thanksgiving dinner for the homeless," says Randy White, senior pastor at Without Walls International Church. "Now that we have the space to do it in our own yard, we'd like to find a way to bus them here for the party."

The Whites, who came to Tampa thirteen years ago, say they sometimes worried they wouldn't have rent money after they started their church in 1991.

Last year, they claimed a combined income of $600,000. Of that, $179,000 is Randy White's annual salary from Without Walls, a church that claims fifteen thousand members and brings in $10 million yearly in revenues. Co-pastor Paula White, who is gaining international acclaim as a televangelist and speaker, is paid $120,000. They also receive an $80,000 housing allowance from the church. Their ministry owns a jet airplane, a Cadillac Escalade and a Mercedes-Benz sedan.

The Whites did not reveal whether they had borrowed funds from their ministry to purchase their home.[74]

They're Leavin' On a Jet Plane:[75]

ENTRY-LEVEL, STARTER JETS
Up-and-coming Tilton impersonator Paula White owns a Hawker-Siddeley "Jet Dragon"—aptly named for the trail of smoke it would leave IF it could fly or IF she could get parts for this 1965-vintage relic. Truly a vanity purchase, it's been grounded since she bought it, just so she can SAY she has a jet.

THE CESSNA CITATION CLUB
Copeland protégés Jesse Duplantis and Jerry Savelle, plus Florida upstart Mark Bishop, each fly their own Cessna Citation 500. They cruise at four hundred miles per hour with a range of 1,400 miles and carry a price tag of about $1.25 million each.

THE GRUMMAN GULFSTREAM GUYS
Fred Price, Creflo Dollar and Brother Benny Hinn all have their own Grumman Gulfstream II's. With a two-man crew and nineteen passengers, these babies cruise at 581 mph with a range of 4,275 miles. Used, they're worth about $4.5 million each.

THE BIG-BUCK BOYS, THE CHALLENGER 600s

Paul Crouch owns the current Queen of the Flying-Televangelist Fleet—a Bombardier Challenger 604. Carrying a crew of two plus nineteen passengers, she cruises at 529 mph with a range of 3,860 miles. She's valued at $16.5 million, not including Paul's "special interior remodeling."

The late Ken Hagin's Challenger 601, about ten years older than Paul's, is "only" worth about $9.6 million.

Joyce Meyer has her own Challenger 600. A full eighteen years older than Paul's, this one's only worth a paltry $4.5 million. Let's hear it for Joyce's frugal stewardship!

KENNY COPELAND—UNDISPUTED KING OF THE FLYING COWBOYS

His Cessna Citation 550 Bravo (valued at $3.4 million), PLUS his Grumman Gulfstream II (worth $4.5 million) AND his Cessna Golden Eagle AND his Beech E-55 AND his assorted lesser aircraft AND his own airport all add up to untold millions of poor folks' dollars. But Kenny's masterstroke is the fact that he's now telling the faithful that God wants him and wife Gloria to EACH have their own Cessna Citation Ten super-jets. Flying just below the speed of sound, these state-of-the-art flying palaces carry a base sticker price of $20 million! That means when "God" has his way, the widows and orphans will have "invested" just about $50-60 million in Kenny's Heavenly Air Force.

UPDATE: "Over the past several years Kenneth and Gloria Copeland have been believing God for a Cessna Citation X jet—a plane they would be able to use in fulfilling their God-appointed assignment and the calling on Kenneth Copeland Ministries to take the Word of God to the world—from the top to the bottom and all the way around. At 2 p.m. on Friday, July 22, 2005, we made the initial deposit and signed the order for Citation X #240. We will take delivery on the plane the first week of March 2006"!

Conclusion

There are bound to be some people who will read this article and say to themselves, "So the leadership lives in nice houses or nice areas, so what? This is God's way of blessing them. They deserve this for leading God's people." I wonder if these people ever really stop to think about what they are saying. Do they really believe that God would bless those in leadership with lifestyles that totally contradict everything that Jesus taught. He and the men who led the first century church led by example. They were servant leaders. Ask yourself if any of the apostles would've chosen pricey homes or affluent areas for themselves. More to the point, would Jesus have done so? Ask yourself if the apostles would have used the contributions and tithes of the people in order to have done so? More to the point, would Jesus have done so?"[76]

CHAPTER 9

PROPHETS, PRIESTS AND PRETENDERS

"If truth were self-evident, eloquence would not be necessary."
—Cicero

Far too often many preachers pride themselves on their candidness. "I say what I please," or "I say what I believe is right," they boast. Most have a very high opinion of themselves, and that all the truth is theirs. This frankness can be a great virtue coupled with humility and intelligence, and in the hands of the right individual. The majority of time, however, ministers in the pulpit, and especially on television, do not follow the advice of James the Apostle:

> *"Even so the tongue is a little member, and boasteth great things. Behold, how great a matter a little fire kindleth! And the tongue is a fire, a world of iniquity: so is the tongue among our members, that it defileth the whole body, and setteth on fire the course of nature; and it is set on fire of hell."*
> —James 3:5,6

We have lost the concept of grandeur just when the forces of religion are making vast gains and the churches are more prosperous than ever before. She has surrendered her once noble concept of God and substituted for it a low, sordid view, unworthy of responsible, worshipping men. Unbelieving men and women have engrossed secular affairs indifferent to Christ, to the world to come, and sought their own selfish ends. "One cannot long read the scriptures sympathetically without noticing the radical disparity between the outlook of men of the Bible and that of modern men. We are today suffering from a secularized mentality. Where the sacred writers saw God, we see the laws of nature. Their world was fully populated; ours is all but empty. Their world was alive and personal; ours is personal and dead. God ruled their world; ours is ruled by the laws of nature and we are always once removed from the presence of God."[77] Grass-roots spirituality has been swallowed up by its own success. Priests, ministers, and rabbis have humanized institutional religion and flooded society with tapes, seminars, and videos—to one end and that is to make money. yhe idea has worked well, for Americans are more religious today that ever before—at least they are on Sunday. Visibly our clergymen resemble actors or salesmen, congregations mirror theaters and civic clubs, and our worship services have the makings of a rock concert.

"Anointing"

Webster defines anointing as "to choose by or as if by divine election." In other words, being anointed has the connotation of having something special from God. Many televangelists, especially those on Trinity Broadcasting Network, expound this philosophy—they are using psychology to enhance your religious feelings. John Hagee and T.D. Jakes—who both carry a lot of weight, in more ways than one—strut the stage like prideful peacocks expounding their anointing, often pausing for the audience to clap in recognition of their great oratory. And if this presentation makes you feel good, then clap louder for more of the same. The real world begins on Monday morning, and with this superficial high received on Sunday, the ecstasy is soon lost. Remember, Christianity is not momentary exuberance of shouting and hand waving, or rolling in the aisles, but an inward and real joy of Christ's presence in their life. The secular world and real life is not always a rosy picture—death, pain, injustice, fear, starvation abounds. True religion will help you over the bumps of life, while chaotic religious frenzies soon become a thing of the past.

> *"Peace I leave with you, my peace I give unto you: not as the world giveth, give I unto you. Let not your heart be troubled, neither let it be afraid."*
> —John 14:27

"Healing and Tongues"

When Oral Roberts broke ties with the Methodist Association some fifty years ago and joined hands among the Pentecostals, no one dreamed of the impact on religion that would ensue. Television healing programs have become frontrunners among evangelicals and charismatics alike. At his retirement Oral passed the baton to his son Richard, and boy, did he run with it. Richard Roberts and his second wife, Lindsay, are experts at appealing to the emotions of people. Americans want to punish their bodies through improper diets or lack of exercise, and then be healed instantly when they become ill. Oral and Richard Roberts, Benny Hinn, Rodney Howard-Browne, Morris Cerullo, and many others will attempt to oblige them, while building their own empire and egos at the same time.

Do people who are sick actually get divine healing by means of so-called "faith healers?" Some do, but most often the sickness is in their mind. The Bible is very clear to God's plan for physical healing—all cases being private, not for public ecstasy or display.

> *"Is any among you afflicted? let him pray. Is any merry? let him sing psalms. Is any sick among you? let him call for the elders of the church; and let them pray over him, anointing him with oil in the name of the Lord: and the prayer of faith shall save the sick, and the Lord shall raise him up; and if he has committed, they shall forgive him."*
> —James 5:13-15

Dr. Robert L. Hughes, president of a theological seminary and a dear friend, once told me this story. "Tom," he said, "many years ago I attended a healing revival in southern Indiana with some fellow students, while in seminary. Near the end of the service a middle-aged gentleman came down the aisle on crutches. Just prior to reaching the pulpit, he threw down his crutches, shouted for joy, and ran back up the aisle and out the tent. The preacher said, 'Praise God,' and passed the offering plate." Dr. Hughes then continued: "Several days prior to the revival I, by chance, ventured upon this same individual on crutches near a cattle farm. A fully mature Black Angus bull guarding some females began to chase the gentleman, and again with the same results, he threw down his crutches and ran." Now, tell me, where is the faith and the healing?

Real or imaginary so-called "healing services" do garner a large following with great interest. This form of religious ecstasy—tongue speaking being another—are experiences that one can share with others for personal edification and gratification. "If it feels good, do it," so to speak. However, with the vast majority being phony, one has to have a larger and larger dosage of this religious ecstasy just to maintain the current level of excitement. It has similarities to taking drugs or to pagan worship.

"Pride"

We are always shocked when we hear of a pastor or televangelist who has used their position for sinful gain. Rightly so! Spiritual maturity should be evidenced in ethical behavior. But we must equally apply this principle to all believers. We are all gifted by God for ministry. We have all received the Spirit empowering us for ministry. It is always wrong when we use claimed spirituality as a cloak for sin."[78] This truth not only applies to preachers, but any church member who professes Christianity and spirituality for personal gain.

In our society of "pampered saints" the plight of contemporary man is often seen in his striving for the road of self-gratification. God is not now, nor has He ever been, looking for credentials to carry on His work.

Our pulpits today are filled with athletes, celebrities, and sundry other personalities who want to sell you their viewpoint on the "Christian experience," while simultaneously trying to alleviate you of your wallet. In today' s tempestuous world God does not need men and women with medals or trophies—but for scars. Warriors who are disciplined, battle-ready, tried and true!

> *"For though we walk in the flesh, we do not war after the flesh: for the weapons of our warfare are not carnal, but mighty through God to the pulling down of strongholds; casting down imaginations, and every high thing that exalteth itself against the knowledge of God, and bringing into captivity every thought to the obedience of Christ; and having in a readiness to revenge all disobedience, when your obedience is fulfilled."*
> —II Corinthians 10:3-6

Pride is considered by many to be the greatest of all sins. This in essence is a truth because: pride takes you farther than you want to go, keeps you longer than you want to stay, and costs you far more than you have means to pay. Many preachers and believers alike have found this to be all to real, but most notably with preachers numerous other lives are affected.

> *"Pride goeth before destruction, and a haughty spirit before a fall."*
> —Proverbs 16:18

Jim Bakker was one of these infamous casualties, when in March of 1987 he stepped down as PTL president and chairman after acknowledging a 1980 extramarital sexual encounter with a secretary. A subsequent agreement of $265,000 from donations to the ministry was made to Jessica Hahn to quiet her complaints. In the end, however, the lid came off, and Bakker served six years in the penitentiary for misappropriating funds towards a lavish lifestyle.

Likewise Jimmy Swaggart, who portrayed himself a saint—free from sin and the epitome of religious ideals—fell from grace after being instrumental in pulling the plug on Bakker. He often enjoyed the company of prostitutes himself. Swaggart confessed his sin only after photographs were presented by Marvin Gorman to the officials of the Assemblies of God. Furthermore, after a period of reconciliation he was caught again, this time by policemen, driving down a one-way street—the wrong way—in a friend's white Jaguar with another prostitute.

> *"He that covereth his sins shall not prosper: but whosoever confesseth and forsaketh them shall have mercy."*
> —Proverbs 28:13

"A Self Examination"

These are the twenty-two questions the members of John Wesley's Holy Club[79] asked themselves each day in their private devotions over two hundred years ago:

1. Am I consciously or unconsciously creating the impression that I am better than I really am? In other words, or do I exaggerate?
2. Am I honest in all my acts and words, or do I exaggerate?
3. Do I confidently pass on to another what was told me in confidence?
4. Can I be trusted?
5. Am I a slave to dress, friends, or work habits.
6. Am I self-conscious, self-pitying, or self-justifying?
7. Did the Bible live in me today?
8. Do I give it time to speak to me every day?
9. Am I enjoying prayer?
10. When did I last speak to someone else of my faith?
11. Do I pray about the money I spend?
12. Do I get to bed on time and get up0 on time?
13. Do I disobey God in anything?

14. Do I insist upon doing something about which my conscience is uneasy?
15. Am I defeated in any part of my life?
16. Am I jealous, impure, critical, irritable, touchy, or distrustful?
17. How do I spend my spare time?
18. Am I proud?
19. Do I thank God that I am not as other people, especially as the Pharisee who despised the publican.
20. Is there anyone whom I fear, dislike, disown, criticize, resent, or disregard? If so, what am I doing about it?
21. Do I grumble or complain constantly?
22. Is Christ real to me?

Question: "How many spiritual leaders fit into this mold today? None!!!"

Almost 100 percent of the time, evangelical leaders take on the role of a celebrity, and not the religious ideals to which they are called. This is because traditional sainthood takes a lifetime of effort and endurance, while the evangelical celebrity earns the title quickly through entrepreneurial energy and personal charisma.

Should fallen preachers or spiritual leaders be restored to their original position? This question is often debated and talked upon with little and often varying results. My answer is a resounding "no!" This is substantiated by the Biblical qualifications of a pastor, bishop, and elder.

"This is a true saying, if a man desire the office of a bishop, he desireth a good work. A bishop then must be BLAMELESS, the HUSBAND of one wife, vigilant, sober, of GOOD behavior, given to hospitality, apt to teach; not given to wine, no striker, not GREEDY of filthy lucre; but patient, not a brawler, not COVETOUS."
—I Timothy 3:1-3

"If any be blameless, the HUSBAND of one wife, having faithful children not accused of riot or unruly. For a bishop must be blameless, as the steward of God; not self-willed, not soon angry, not given to wine, no striker, not given to filthy LUCRE."
—Titus 1:6,7

These words are the canon of evangelicals and televangelists. So, move over Paula White and Joyce Meyer; you and others are in it for the fame and fortune.

"Prince of the Air"

"For we wrestle not against flesh and blood, but against principalities, against powers, against the rulers of the darkness of this world, against spiritual wickedness in high places."
—Ephesians 6:12

The devil, Satan, is recognized by Jesus as the prince of this world (John 14:30). Thus, it is not hard to understand why the world is so alienated towards God, to His Son, and to His commandments. Also, why America harbors a meteoric rise in cults, in astrology, ESP, Satan worship, black magic, and witchcraft. All these, however, involve individuals or small groups of people confined into small arenas. An ambitious and wise devil seeks to pervert nations, control governments, and deceive Christly principles. His main goal is to denigrate the Church, the bride of Christ, into a worldly ecclesiasticism. This has mostly been accomplished by hoarding and misuse of money.

"False Prophets"

"For such are false apostles, deceitful workers, transforming themselves into the apostles of Christ. And no marvel; for Satan himself is transformed into an angel of light."
—II Corinthians 11:13,14

Every group of people, no matter how large or how small has someone set aside as their leader. A boy scout troop has a scoutmaster, the women's garden club has their president, and the church has a pastor, an elder, or a bishop. These individuals are looked up to and naturally carry the most influence; their thoughts and actions portray that of their followers. Many people are sincere about what they do and believe; however, the vast majority are sincerely wrong. I read about the Supreme Court decision of the state of New York concerning the actions of the Reverend Sun Myung Moon. Basically, the decision handed down was that, if Mr. Sun Moon was sincere in his beliefs then these beliefs are justified. Well, I could be sincere in robbing a bank to buy food for my family, but I would be sincerely wrong.

> Jesus said, *"Many will say to me in that day, Lord, Lord, have we not prophesied in thy name? And in thy name have cast out devils? And in thy name done many wonderful works? And then will I profess unto them, I never knew you: depart from me, you that work iniquity."*
> —Matthew 7:22,23

Here Jesus is talking about false prophets. He said, "beware of false prophets." As a young boy it was natural for me to think of preachers, all preachers, as good and godly people. The fact remains; however, that most preachers are gainful people living for self and their families. They have little interest in the Lord. They are the devil's angels in a black suit carrying the Black Book.

"Fleecing the Sheep"

> *"Lord, grant that I may seek rather to comfort, than to be comforted—to understand, than to be understood—to love, than to be loved—for it is by giving that one receives."*
> —St. Francis of Assisi

Recent Internal Revenue Service figures show that Americans who earn the most contribute the smallest percentage of their income to charity. Those earning $10,000 to $15,000 donated an average of $725 last year, while those earning $40,000 to $50,000 contributed $950. The vast majority of these low wage earners are widows and the elderly on fixed incomes. They spend a great deal of time at home and become exploited by televangelists and petitioners by mail—particularly at Christmas.

Many charities live or die on contributions during the Christmas season—hoping for increased generosity. But be cautious. While most are legitimate and worthy of support suggests the national Council of Better Business Bureaus, there are always unscrupulous folks who prey on holiday feelings. Plan your giving, says the council, and always—without fail—demand accountability of the group receiving your gift.

"Selling Religion"

The following is a letter written three years ago to *Dear Abby* by a lady in Wisconsin concerning a renown TV "faith healing" evangelist.

"Dear Abby: I have a problem that is eating my insides out. I started writing to a TV evangelist because I have multiple sclerosis. I know he is well-respected, in touch with God and does many good things. The problem is that he always wants more money. I sent him $100. Then he wrote to me personally and told me that something great was going to happen to me, but I had to send him another $100 first—even if I had to save my pennies and get the money any way I could!

I believe in God with all my heart and strive to be a good person, but Abby, I can't take food from my children's mouths because this man says God will do something good for me if I do. That comes very close to saying that God can be bought.

My husband is very angry with me because I sent as much as I did. I would like to be free of my disease, but I will not deny my family the necessities in order to send this man money.

I'm beginning to believe that all they want is my money—money that I don't have. God understands. Why can' t they?

HOSPITAL FOR SINNERS

> *"He hath showed thee, O man, what is good; and what doth the Lord require of thee, but to do justly, and to love mercy, and to walk humbly with thy God?"*
>
> —Micah 6:8

"Religious Fidelity"

Webster defines "deceive" as "to make a person believe what is not true: delude, mislead." It implies "deliberate misrepresentation of facts by words or actions to further one's ends." The Bible also gives strong and direct warnings against deceptions. For example, I Corinthians 15:33, Galatians 6:7-8, and I John 1:6 are just a few of Scriptural passages denouncing this abomination.

John C. Baldwin, former president of the North American Securities Administrators Association, has said, "beware of the growing number of investment con artists who are out to fleece the flocks of the faithful." Mr. Baldwin has expressed his frustration about church members that do not take action against "con artists" and for their lack of cooperation with law-enforcement officials investigating the frauds.

According to the latest survey, investment schemes have cost more than 15,000 Americans a total of $450 million in the last five years. This, however, is only a percentage of the entire picture because the survey involved only fifteen states. In one case alone, Stephen Streit, a treasurer of the largest Baptist church in Alabama, took $18 million from 193 investors, and one of these was an unidentified member of Congress. To be somewhat comforting, reported one victim, Mr. Streit included Bible verses at the end of monthly statements. He is now serving ten years in jail.

"Pastor on a Pedestal"

Sebring, Florida, a small community nestled between glittering lakes and orange groves, is where the Reverend John Canning wove his spells like an ancient soothsayer.

"To his mostly elderly parishioners, he was a trusted caretaker, a vigorous man of God, a speaker who laid his hand on the Holy Writ and told the truth," reports *The Orlando Sentinel* in March 1995.

But over the course of the past two months, Florida investigators say that Reverend Canning not only laid his hands on the Word of God but also on tens of thousands of dollars belonging to a 90-year-old church couple.

Leo and Hazel Gleese, who had once asked the 58-year-old preacher to be their adopted son, lost their money, a second home, and eventually their lives to this spinner of spiritual tales. Pastor John Canning is now in jail for strangling and beating in the faces of the Gleeses with a cane.

These recent events of fraud and deceit have led to much head shaking in Sebring, a community of eleven thousand, about ninety miles south of Orlando. And Canning wasn't the only minister arrested last week.

Donald Johnson, a minister of the First Church of God, was charged with nearly thirty counts of sexual misconduct involving adults and children. It was a great week for preachers in and around Sebring.

> *"It is better to trust in the Lord than to put confidence in man."*
> —Psalm 118:8

"Professional Cons"

They are often called boiler room operations. Specifically—they are professional solicitors using the telephone to drum up money for charities. The term boiler room originated "because it used to be illegal," said Fran Stephanz, executive director of the Better Business Bureau. "They used to get into dark cellars—where nobody could hear them—literally boiler rooms."

But today, this type of operation is legal. Professional solicitors rent office space, install some twenty or so telephones, and begin making appeals for donations to charity.

The solicitor and the charity have a contract. The charity usually gets the least amount—sometimes thirty percent; sometimes twenty percent; and sometimes even ten percent. "I've known cases where the charity has actually come out with nothing before—and that's not illegal, said Jim Morano, coordinator for the charitable solicitations department of the state Office of Consumer Affairs in Richmond, Virginia.

There are numerous solicitor groups across the United States who come to a state, set up, sell tickets for a charity and leave with the money, or sell advertising but never print a program. They don't have a home office—so they cannot be found to be prosecuted. Therefore, in reality, the telephone solicitations are predominately a commercial operation in that the charity gets such a small percentage of the money.

"Food Shortage"

Recently the prime minister of one of the African nations said he believed that Americans have a distorted view of Africa. Charitable organizations with the aid of television tends to make us believe the entire continent is starving. This is not the case. It is true; however, that in years of drought and famine starvation does occur, but not to the extent we are made to believe.

In fact, Third World food scarcity was quite new until the 1970's. The late 1960's had been good years for agriculture throughout the world. Grain production was up, more than outdistancing population in both developing and developed countries. New high-yielding varieties of grains were coming into their own.

If anything has hurt world production and caused starvation, it has been bad economics by greedy people—raising the costs of production machinery and fuel. As a result there has been some famine and starvation; only to be exploited by "money hungry" charitable organizations.

Have you ever witnessed on TV or received a letter in the mail accompanied by a picture or two of starving refugees in Africa or India? Depressing and emotionally upsetting indeed. I am often moved with much compassion—exactly what the projection is intended to accomplish. Many charitable organizations use this type of psychology for selfish reasons and monetary gain. Red-tape, unusual high salaries, and over- expenditures commonly prevent the "needy" from reaping the benefits. And in many cases, when an organization sends you a couple of pictures, these are the only two they support. A friend in another state and myself proved this- -we both received the same pictures of the needy children.

> *"For they that are such serve not our Lord Jesus Christ, but their own belly; and by good words and fair speeches deceive the hearts of the simple."*
> —Romans 16:18

The following is a letter I received from an organization seeking to raise money by offering a sweepstakes.

> "Yet some will die, needlessly and helplessly of preventable disease, neglect and hunger, unless you help NOW! Your donation of $100, $50, $25 or whatever you can afford will bring health, education, and a new-life to people now without hope. Your tickets are enclosed and each has a different number. One of these may make you a winner of a late model car or truck of your choice—to be given as a prize."

There is a flood of people and organizations today who appear deeply interested in starving children around the world. Yet, there seems to be little concern for their neighbor next door, or maybe, down the street. Could it be that there is no monetary gain in this type of endeavor for themselves?

"World Vision"

Bob Pearce founded World Vision back in the 1940's and directed this organization with honor and dignity. World Vision, under Bob's leadership, was the pioneer and forerunner of all other charitable organizations. Through the years, however, this once great institution has become carnal and selfish in scope and vision. Movie stars and personalities are now pocketing the greatest percentage of the donations.

Personal missionary friends of mine—now serving or have served in Africa—tell me similar organizations like Save the Children, Children International, or the American Red Cross, are not faring much better. Again we have promotional fees, high salaries, and excessive paperwork taking the profits. Generally we find only ten to twenty percent of the total amount ever getting out of this country.

> *"Feed the flock of God which is among you, taking the oversight thereof, not by constraint, but willingly; not for filthy lucre, but of a ready mind."*
> —I Peter 5:2

A once prominent catholic missions program in upstate New York, served three dozen countries until it was revealed that the priests were enjoying communion and the company of nuns a little too much. Abstinence had given way to wine, women, and song.

The following is a letter I received some ten years ago from this organization, soliciting funds for the needy.

> "The scenes of starvation and death are horrible in the Sub-Sahara region of Africa. The desert has been creeping south—slowly and pitilessly, bringing hunger, starvation and death—relentlessly.
>
> There has been a prolonged period of drought, an invasion of plant-eating locusts, and disease spreading rampantly. The people affected—some twenty million live in straw covered shacks, eat anything from roots to rats, and have no medical aid.
>
> One thousand deaths a day, every day, month after month, have already yielded half a million corpses. Typhoid, dysentery, and flies are spreading at a menacing pace.

Can you send the price of a cup of coffee per day? Many of you can even send $25 or $50 per month. Please HELP!"

My advice to everyone who asks me about charities is: first, find out the bottom line—how much of the actual donation goes to charity; and second, call the Better Business Bureau for information. Never, never give money over the telephone, or to solicitors on street corners. Unless, perhaps, it is the Salvation Army. This charitable organization is still doing the right job.

> *"Riches are the least worthy gifts which God can give us...yet we toil for them day and night, and take no rest. Therefore God frequently gives riches to foolish people, to whom he gives nothing else."*
> —Martin Luther

CHAPTER 10

TRUE SAMARITAN

"You can give without loving, however, you cannot love without giving."

—Old Adage

Too many pastors in America are all too ready and excited about taking an offering in order to keep the machine works of a church running in high gear. In contrast, far too few are willing to pass the plate for the needy. Wealthy Christians and church members are often hesitant and unwilling to help the poor, but will often say: "God will bless you" or "I will pray for you." Keep your prayers for God does not hear you anyway. Prayer comes cheap for it costs the wealthy nothing.

How many times have you seen people at intersections holding up various signs: "need money for food" or "need money for medicine"? How many times have you seen them and passed them by? You often conclude in your mind that he or she wants money for beer, wine, or cigarettes. Well, maybe! We as humans do not know the true answer. Some of these people really do need help. What is the solution? Stop! Offer these individuals five dollars, or ten dollars, or whatever, and say, "Take this money in the name of Jesus." This frees you of any responsibility when and if the money is misused. You have portrayed the "true Samaritan."

Parable of the Good Samaritan

"No one is useless in the world who
lightens the burden of it for anyone else."
—Charles Dickens

The story of The Good Samaritan is a parable appearing only in the Gospel of Luke (10:25-37). Jesus told this parable to illustrate how compassion is necessary for all people, and that engaging or fulfilling the spirit of the Law is far more important than emphasizing the letter of the Law.

This parable is important, as it is famous because generous people should be ready and willing to furnish aid to people in poverty without hesitation or reservation. This is a universal moral law. We should help anyone in need; not merely people of the same faith or same church. It takes true compassion to give to someone who cannot return the favor.

"Mother Teresa"

Mother Teresa, the missionary nun once said: "To me, God and compassion are one and the same. Just a smile, or carrying a bucket of water, or showing some simple kindness. These small things make up compassion. Compassion means trying to share and understand the suffering of people. In addition, I think it is very good when people suffer. To me, that is really like the kiss of Jesus. It is a sign that this person has come very close to Jesus and sharing His passion. When we ultimately go home to God, we are going to be judged on what we were to each other, what we did for each other, and, especially, how much love we put in that. It 's not how much we give, but how much love we put in the doing—that's compassion in action."[80]

"The only way to have a friend is to be one."
—Ralph Waldo Emerson

"Habitat for Humanity"

Biblically speaking the only reason for seeking wealth is to share with the needy and give to the poor. This is what Jesus told the rich young ruler; he departed saddened because he had great wealth. His heart was in the riches amassed in his life. Religious leaders today seek and attain great wealth. They continually "fleece the sheep" for their own lifestyles and goals.

A person's faith needs to be demonstrated and shared in order to accomplish effectiveness. Let us see how a millionaire became a Good Samaritan and founded Habitat for Humanity in 1976.

Before starting one of the world's most successful programs, Millard Fuller was a millionaire more concerned about speedboats and fancy cars then his faith.

"Things got pushed ahead of my devotion to Christ," said Fuller, the founder of Habitat for Humanity. "I never abandoned the church. But I became primarily interested in getting an education and making money."

A crisis erupted with my wife leaving," said Fuller, father of four children. "I had not only abandoned God, but my family as well." After reflecting on his situation, Fuller reconciled with his wife Linda and began his search to find out what God wanted him to do. Fuller gave up his business, sold his possessions and gave the money to the poor.

"I don't advocate that a businessperson can't be a good Christian," Fuller said. "I would say if your overriding satisfaction in life is to make money, then you're in spiritual trouble."

Fuller and his wife moved to a Christian community near Americus, Georgia, and started building houses for low-income families on a nonprofit, no-interest basis. They tested the program for three years in Africa before coming back to the U.S. and founding Habitat for Humanity in 1976.

From the outset, Fuller wanted Habitat for Humanity to be an ecumenical symbol of faith in action.

"Churches are different," Fuller said. "What we are trying to do at Habitat for Humanity is acknowledge the fact that there are theological differences, but we can agree on a hammer and use it to build a house for a family and fulfill the rule of Christ."

That "rule" involves more than just going to church every Sunday, Fuller said.

"We say it's fine to go to church, but you assemble yourself together for a purpose—and that purpose is to be inspired and equipped to go outside of the church and do something."

When Fuller is not traveling, he attends Maranatha Baptist Church in Plains, Georgia.

Maranatha Baptist's most famous member, Jimmy Carter, invited Fuller into the Southern Baptist congregation when they were working together on a housing project about eight years ago.

"He told me, 'Look, you recruited me for Habitat for Humanity, I want to recruit you as a member of my church,'" Fuller said.

Fuller occasionally substitutes for Carter when the former president is too busy resolving political crises to teach Sunday school at the church.

But Habitat is clearly at the core of Fuller's religious work. He stresses that God's first commandment is not, "go to church every Sunday."

"The first commandment is to love God with all your strength and to love your neighbor as yourself," said Fuller, adding that true Christianity is about helping those people no one else wants to help.

"Jesus lined up the harlots and lepers," Fuller said. "For someone that seriously wants to follow Christ, we have to look at Jesus for who he really was—not the sugarcoated version of what we've made him up to be."

Habitat for Humanity is true evangelism because it changes lives, Fuller said.

"I think it's evangelical in the deepest sense of the word," he said. "A lot of people think evangelism is passing out Bible tracts and loudly expressing belief in Christ. True evangelism is that message that penetrates into the heart of a person."

Fuller has already visited Ethiopia and Egypt to promote low-income housing this year and has another trip planned to New Zealand.

Fuller will return to Lynchburg this fall when churches supporting Lynchburg Habitat for Humanity will build nineteen new houses on Bright Star Court off Florida Avenue.

"It's unusual for me to go to the same place twice in one year," Fuller said. "But the Lynchburg affiliate, which is one of thirty-two affiliates in Virginia, is not only one of the finest Habitat affiliates in the state, but is one of the finest affiliates in the nation and the world."

Today, this nonprofit organization has built more than 200,000 homes for the poor and needy. The houses were built with no profit added and no interest charged. The organization believes that the poor do not need charity but capital, not caseworkers but coworkers. How about you? The conservative religious right needs to give a helping hand, not a hand to help themselves.

> *"No Christian has a right to the luxury of contentment when he knows that poverty, hunger and disease are rampant in his neighborhood, nation and world."*
> —Harry Emerson Fosdick

"Poor and Homeless"

It is a lot easier to think that people who are getting assistance are lazy. Many people lose their jobs for one reason or another; and usually end up having to work a much lower paying job. Prices on goods—especially gas—continually rise, while many workers find their wages, benefits, and insurance decline.

The following excerpt from *Parade Magazine* by Colin Greer helps portray some of the poverty in America. Everyone wants the government to find a solution; however, our churches need to take the responsibility.

"Sometimes I don't have enough to feed the whole family," said Sandra of McClellanville, SC. "I feed my three children first, and then I'll go without a meal." Sandra has completed two years of college and now works full-time for a social-services agency for about $12,000 a year. "We're hungry," she said, "but we're not starving. It's a real battle."

When Americans think of starving people, they think of Third World countries. But what many people don't realize, says Robert Fersh, president of the Food Research and Action Center (FRAC), a nonprofit organization working to alleviate hunger, is that millions of people endure hunger right here at home. Parents are going to bed without food so they can feed their children. Baby formula is mixed with water to make it last longer. People are eating rice and beans, because there isn't enough money for groceries at the end of the month.

Over the next few months, the question of hunger will dominate the welfare-reform debate, as Congressional committees hear testimony on hunger and federal food-assistance programs.

The Action Center reports that more than five million children under twelve go hungry each month. Last October, the U.S. Census Bureau acknowledged that 39.3 million Americans, or about fifteen percent of our population, lived in poverty in 1993.

The federal government considers a family of four to be in poverty if its total annual income is $14,800 or less. If the same family earns $27,380, it is considered low-income. The government uses these definitions to determine the level of assistance a family receives in various welfare and food programs. (Almost 90% of families on welfare also receive food stamps.) Nearly forty-two percent of American children grow up in low-income families, and about 23%—almost one child in four—grow up in poverty. This is double the child-poverty rate of any other industrialized country.

Not surprisingly, the strongest predictor of hunger is poverty.

The Food Research and Action Center is a legal advocacy group created in 1970 to represent the concerns of classes of citizens who could not defend their own interests (another example is the Children's Defense Fund). Originally financed by the federal government, it is now supported by such foundations as Ford and Prudential. FRAC regularly reviews upcoming legislation that affects the hungry. "An important part of the Action Center's work," says Robert Fersh, a lawyer who previously was the staff director of a House Subcommittee on Nutrition that was chaired by Leon Panetta, "is to discover the extent of hunger in America, to educate Americans about what we find and to coordinate an effective response to eradicate hunger and malnutrition. Policy-makers need to know the extent of hunger in America."

In 1984, the Action Center convened a group of scientists who developed the Community Childhood Hunger Identification Project, or CCHIP (pronounced, "chip"), to scientifically document hunger in America. Seven sites were included in the initial study: Alabama, California, Connecticut, Florida, Michigan, Minnesota and New York.

The Hunger Project's second study will be released next month (the first was released in 1991). Eleven more sites in nine states—Indiana, Maine, New York, Pennsylvania, Utah, Kansas, Ohio, South Carolina and Texas—and Washington, DC, were added this time.

"We took great care in designing our survey and carrying it out," said Cheryl Wehler, the project's director, who received her Ph.D. in nutritional biochemistry from MIT "We hired the same consultant to design our survey who works on surveys for the Department of Health and Human Services and the National Census Bureau. We interviewed more than 8000 low-income families in communities from every region of the U.S. [Most national polls interview far fewer people. For instance, the Gallup Organization, one of the leading national polling services, uses a basic sample of about one thousand people.] We chose sites that represent the national variation of population size, proportion of population living in urban and rural areas, and different racial and ethnic groups.

"We wanted to know not only what hunger looks like in America but also how it looks in a region and in a specific community," added Wehler. "This type of specificity takes a lot of legwork."

People already working to combat poverty in community-based groups—many of them in or close to poverty themselves did that legwork. Cheryl Wehler and her assistant taught these individuals interview techniques to implement the extensive, 165-question survey. "The response rate has been phenomenal—805," said Wehler. "The people interviewed really wanted to help others understand what it is like to be hungry and what they have to go through daily."

To qualify for the study, a household had to be considered low-income and include at least one child under age twelve. A computer program was used to randomly select qualifying households. A family was defined as hungry if it experienced at least five of eight indicators of hunger in the last twelve months. They included:

- Does your household ever run out of money to buy food to make a meal?

- Do you ever cut the size of meals or skip meals because there is not enough money for food?

- Do you ever rely on a limited number of foods to feed your children because you are running out of money to buy food for a meal?

- Do any of your children ever go to bed hungry because there is not enough money to buy food?

"The last week of the month is a real juggling act," says George Garrett (pictured on the cover) of Mulberry, Kansas. He is the father of George Jr., 5, and Kayla, 6. His family lives in the same three-bedroom house in which George grew up. "We eat a lot of beans, and sometimes there's no fresh bread or milk for our kids," he said.

George, 50, worked for twenty-five years as an auto mechanic before he had two heart attacks in the last three years. His wife, Kelly, 28, is in a job-training program. "I want my children to eat well," he said. "We get scared wondering where the next dollar will come from."

For three years, the Garrett family has received Aid to Families with Dependent Children—what most people mean when they talk about welfare-and food stamps. They now get $454 in aid and $311 in food stamps each month. (Federal statistics show that two-thirds of welfare recipients in 1993 were children—9.5 million out of 14.1 million people.)

"On TV and around, you hear people making fun of people on welfare and getting so mad about it," George said. "It's like racism—judging people by the surface. Maybe people get sick, lose their job, lose their house—they can't afford to buy food, and their kids suffer. It's what happened to me."

The U.S. Census Bureau reports that more than one million Americans fell into poverty in 1993. Since 1990, more than 7 million people have been added to the food-stamp program. One in ten Americans now receives food stamps—with more than half of the food stamps going to feed children.

"Sometimes it's just noodles and bouillon," says Kathleen Krausmann, 41, of McKeesport, PA. "I always worry that the kids aren't getting enough protein and fresh vegetables." Her husband, Gary, 40, works at a video store for $5.50 an hour while Kathleen cares for three young sons, including an 11-year-old at home with cerebral palsy, and a niece. "We get about $175 a month in food stamps," she said, " and I don't know how we'd get by without them. We've needed local programs for food—maybe a turkey and fixings for a holiday—and that really helps. It's nice to know there are people who care."

Like George Garrett, Kathleen is sensitive to the stigma that comes from receiving welfare assistance. "I know that it's easier to think people getting assistance are just lazy," she said, "but we're a working family trying to get by. We just can't make it with all the bills and the cost of food. It just shows you that even if you're working, you may not really be making a living."

In fact, the 1991 Hunger Project study indicates that forty-six percent of hungry households have at least one wage earner. Households like Kathleen's spend an average of 54% of their gross income on shelter costs, compared to the typical American family, which spends twenty percent. The average hungry household is only able to spend sixty-eight cents per person per meal, which turns out to be nearly a third of their gross monthly income.

Susanna, 36, of Garland, TX, had to feed her nine year-old son and four year-old daughter on her husband's $20,000-a-year salary. "My son has asthma and even with insurance, the co-payments and transportation to and from doctors cost a lot of money," she said. "Then there are the rent, utility bills and on and on. For two years, the four of us got by on $100 a month for food. You have to be creative to feed a family for that little. I can make a little bit of hamburger go a long way."

Susanna finally landed a job at a nursing home but still worries about those hard times. "I wonder if my kids were getting the vitamins they needed," she said.

Her fears are not unfounded. Hunger and under-nutrition rob children of their potential, a 1993 Tufts University study concluded, resulting in lost knowledge, brainpower and productivity. Hungry children are more than four times likely to suffer from frequent colds, ear infections and headaches. Hungry children miss school because of sickness more often and, as the Hunger Project found, they go to the doctor almost twice as often.

Monica, 25, from Washington, DC, received assistance from the Women, Infants and Children (WIC) program when she was pregnant with her third child. This program provides nutritious foods, nutrition education and access to health care to low-income women who are pregnant or caring for an infant.

"I don't know how I would have been able to eat properly without it," Monica said. She now works part-time as a cashier and has completed two years of college. "I've been getting help," she said, "but I'm looking forward to getting a degree and having a better life for my three kids and me too."

Poor diet is closely related to low birth weight, which is a factor in the deaths of infants during their first twelve months. Twenty-three other developed nations have lower infant-mortality rates than the United States.

Robert Fersh noted that a Department of Agriculture study found that for every $1 spent on a pregnant woman in its Women, Infants and Children program, $1.77 to $3.13 is saved in Medicaid costs during her child's first sixty days of life.

"If children don't get the nutrition necessary for concentration and learning," Fersh stressed, "America won't get the educated workforce and high productivity it needs.

"The Hunger Project study is a warning."[81]

"Five Steps You Can Take to Help"

1. Volunteer at soup kitchens and food pantries. Offer to help out at the agencies in your area that are combating hunger.

2. Offer to help low-income people fill out the food-stamp application. Many local groups train volunteers to do this.

3. Be an advocate in matters of public policy. Help publicize the facts about anti-hunger programs: Who is eligible, what the programs do and how people who are eligible can use them.

4. Donate money, equipment, materials or food to agencies fighting hunger.

5. Promote self-help projects that cut food costs, such as farmers' markets and community gardens in low-income neighborhoods. Get young people involved as well.[82]

All across America we find that hunger is spilling into the middle class. There is a group of "new poor" emerging, thus, Americans can no longer simply label the poor as lazy and just ignore or forget them.

> *"The poor of the world are the hope of salvation of mankind. We will be judged by what we have done to help them."*
> —Mother Teresa

"Homeless"

Homelessness can be caused by a variety of problems. The main cause is unaffordable housing for the poor. Secondary causes can include mental illness, physical illnesses, substance abuse, lack of incentives to work, poor work ethics, and, like most social issues Grassroots.org seeks to address lack of decent education. The National Law Center for Homelessness and Poverty reports that over three million men, women, and children were homeless over the past year—about thirty percent of them chronically and the others temporarily. In many cases, people are in and out of the homeless system, which includes shelters, hospitals, the streets, and prisons. It is these chronic users of the system that utilize up to 90% of the nation's resources devoted to the problem.

On top of the three million who were homeless or marginally homeless there are an additional five million poor people that spend over half of their incomes on housing, leaving them on the verge of homelessness. A missed paycheck, a health crisis, or an unpaid bill can easily push poor families over the edge into homelessness.

It has been reported that the types of assistance homeless adults felt they needed most were help finding a job, help finding affordable housing, and help paying for housing. However, the main types of assistance they usually received were clothing, transportation and help with public benefits. Few homeless actually receive help finding housing, likely because caregivers know its unaffordable or otherwise unattainable for people of their social status.

A minority of the homeless population is capable but unwilling to work—they may resent the minimal wages they would receive if we did not consider that a minority of the homeless may be inherently "lazy," or substance abuse has made them so. In these cases there is little help the system can offer that will bring about positive social results. In general, we recommend a "tough love" approach wherein able people must work in some capacity to receive the benefits they seek. There is often a gray line between those who are mentally ill, substance abusers, and other disabled homeless. Therefore, it is not easy to classify them into benefit categories or to understand their labor capabilities.

Moreover, there is no one comprehensive system to manage the myriad of services for the homeless, their benefits, and their reintegration into society. We recommend the U.S. [government] and [individual] states move towards a fully integrated computerized system which would make delivering benefits and getting people off the streets more cost effective. Even though documenting people's lives in detail verges on an invasion of privacy, we feel if the U.S. taxpayers need to foot the bill, which they ultimately do, there is no alternative but to build an efficient system with subjective inputs, in order to provide benefits and opportunities based on need.

Most people, including the homeless, are not inherently lazy. However, the U.S. economic system does not adequately support those at the lowest skill levels, even if they are willing to work. This in turn leads to unemployment and millions of "working poor." Incomes for the poorest Americans have not nearly kept pace with rising housing costs. Therefore, millions of hard workers are shut out of the private housing market. Job training, education, trade schools, and other systemic economic incentives and welfare disincentives should be applied with whatever funds are available from foundation or government sources. This will raise income levels overall and make housing more affordable. This, coupled with the benefits poor and homeless receive like Supplemental Security Income (SSI), food stamps, and TANF (welfare), should lower the overall future level of homelessness.

For mayors, city councils, and even homeless providers it may seem that placing homeless people in shelters is the most inexpensive way of meeting basic needs. This is deceptive. The cost of homelessness can be quite high, particularly for those with chronic illnesses. Because they have no regular place to stay, people who are homeless use a variety of public systems in an inefficient and costly way. Preventing a homeless episode, or ensuring a speedy transition in to stable permanent housing can result in a significant overall cost savings. Hospitals, prisons, lost opportunity, and emergency shelter is all very inefficient. According to a U.S. Conference of Mayors, the homeless population is diverse:

- 20 percent work.
- 22 percent are mentally disabled.
- 11 percent are veterans.
- 34 percent are drug or alcohol dependent.

Most people become homeless specifically because they are having a housing crisis, even though they may have other needs for services and increased incomes. It is important to realize that their needs are best met once the family is in permanent housing—not while they are in transitional housing or shelters. Housing must be first if they are expected to develop a sustainable, healthy lifestyle.

Homelessness can often be caused by serious health problems. Likewise, homelessness can cause health problems. Illnesses that are closely associated with homelessness and poverty include tuberculosis, AIDS, malnutrition, and severe dental problems. Other health problems in society such as alcoholism, mental illnesses, and physical disabilities are even more debilitating for the homeless, since they may have no shelter or money to manage the problem. People without shelter could easily get frostbite, get infections, or be victims of violence, even in public shelters. They are also more likely to cohabitate with drug addicts, alcoholics, and/or others with disease.

Each year millions of homeless people in the United States need important health care services but most do not have health insurance or cash to pay for medical care. Finding health care is an enormous challenge for the homeless.[83]

While millions in the United States—the number growing—are without health insurance, enough food, and living in poverty, very few 'so-called' Christians are passing out life preservers. Many of the wealthy are exploiting the poor, instead of offering help. This is true of Paul and Jan Crouch. The following quote from *The Los Angeles Times* sums this up.

I learned from the *Times'* Hot Property column on Sunday that Costa Mesa-based televangelists Jan and Paul Crouch have purchased a $5 million "palatial estate" with nine bathrooms, a climate-controlled WINE cellar, an elevator, six-car garage and tennis court. Jan Crouch had wanted a bigger yard for her dogs.[84]

> *"But many that are first (in this life) shall be last (in the next life); and the last shall be first."*
> —Matthew 19:30

"Widows and Children"

"Pure religion and undefiled before God and the Father is this, to visit the fatherless and widows in their affliction, and to keep himself unspotted from the world."
—James 1:27

If the number of unwed mothers, divorcees with children, and widows were actually known, it would probably stagger the imagination. An educated guess would be several million. Where is the help coming from? Society does not have the answer. Our churches have and still are failing miserably. The following is a true story; only one of many.

I am a 52-year-old mother and married for nearly thirty years. My husband left me for a younger woman and we have started the divorce procedures. My life is in shambles both mentally and physically. I depended so much on him, but now, my life is worse than death. Christians are not concerned. I have sought out more than one dozen churches seeking an outreach program for older divorced people with now avail. No one has even said, "I'm praying for you." The church my husband and I attended for many years did nothing to make me feel loved. However, when things were going well the church welcomed our attendance and, of course, our money.[85]

This is only one of countless true stories in America today. Are we out to help others, or are we out to help ourselves? The vast majority of today's "so-called" Christians and prominent church leaders are really out to help themselves. God help us!

"There is no security on this earth. Only opportunity."
—Douglas MacArthur "

"In Summary"

A number of years ago, I went back to school for three more years and received a seminary degree. I was then licensed and commissioned by my church to become a missionary prison chaplain. I did this because of the command that Jesus gave in Matthew, chapter twenty-five. This was the last part of His Olivet Discourse and He repeated it twice.

1. Feed the hungry.
2. Clothe the naked.
3. Visit the sick.
4. Visit those in prison.

What are you doing? Is your interest in tending the flock, or merely fleecing the sheep?

The words of Jesus: "For I was hungry, and you gave me no meat: I was thirsty, and you gave me no drink: I was a stranger, and you took me not in: naked, and you clothed me not: sick, and in prison, and you visited me not. Then shall He answer them, saying, verily I say unto you, inasmuch as you did it not to one of the least of these, you did it not to me. And these shall go away into everlasting punishment: but the righteous into life eternal (Matthew 25:42-46).

In closing, I would like to say "hats off" to all the volunteers in America. Some of these many individuals risk their lives for absolutely zero monetary gain. Again, I say "Thank You!"

CHAPTER 11

LIBERTY UNIVERSITY: GOD OR MAMMON

"I only regret that I have but one life to lose for my country."
—Nathan Hale

"I submit to you that a man who hasn't found something to die for, is not fit to live."
—Martin Luther King, Jr.

    I returned from Vietnam in the late 1960's with an honorable discharge and soon began searching for a college to get an education and make use of my entitled benefits from the GI Bill. Junior college seemed a practical choice at the time and after two years I set my sights on a four-year institution. What is today Liberty University was co-founded by Dr. Jerry Falwell and Dr. Elmer Towns in 1971. The Liberty University name had a special ring to it, thus, I enrolled in the 1970's and received degrees from the university and seminary. I even worked for the institution a number of years and all total, have a thirty-year ongoing relationship with Liberty.
    Today there is a Liberty Godparent Home, Liberty Christian School, and Liberty Village, a retirement community where Falwell is the spokesman and receives a salary. All of these establishments entail a little bit about religion; however, they are mostly about money—money at the top. Are these organizations about liberty? No! The name is merely a front in order to achieve a certain amount of notoriety. I do not know of one single televangelist—or their children—who fought for America's freedom, and this includes the Falwells. They just make

money at the expense of other people's sons and daughters. Are our religious leaders fence-sitting citizens? Maybe! I believe that at some point in our lives, we are all called upon to "kick-in" and "ante-up" in service to the country in someway or another. Every one of our conservative religious leaders considers themselves pro-Israel. Well, all Israelis are required to serve in the military—for life. This means they are inactive reservists for life. They are always poised and ready to fight if called upon. Should any less be expected of us? Our infamous conservative religious fanatics realize fully that serving their country requires time and energy, and sometimes life and limb. Yet, this level of sacrificial service conflicts with the business plans of the charismatic religious leaders. It would also threaten the continuation of their family legacy as they continue to employ nepotism. Webster defines nepotism as: "Favoritism shown to relatives, especially in appointments to desirable positions. On the Liberty University campus it is commonly stated by staff and faculty that "Falwell operates like the mafia—he keeps it all in the family!" This can easily be accomplished when you are founder, chancellor, and "dictator" of an institution.

> *"They who would give up essential liberty for temporary security, deserve neither liberty nor security."*
> —Benjamin Franklin

"Politics"

Early in his life as pastor of Thomas Road Baptist Church, Falwell sought to move into political activism nationally. Jerry Falwell's explanation of his move to politics seemed simple: "God wanted me to look beyond Lynchburg. We cannot be isolationists. We've got to have the world upon our hearts." Falwell is a fundamentalist. "The entire Bible," he insists, "from Genesis to Revelation, is the inerrant word of God, and totally accurate in all respects." As Falwell reads scripture, "it stands foursquare against abortion, gay rights, feminism, excessive welfare programs, pornography, tolerance of Communist expansion, and

Salt II."[86] However, our dear brother left out involvement in politics as something that scripture is against as well.

"Republican Launching Platform"

Liberty University is used by Jerry Falwell as a springboard for his republican candidates that will endorse the agendas he deems necessary. In fact, several years ago Senator McCain stated that "Falwell was a man of intolerance." Recently, however, Falwell and McCain mended fences and settled differences. McCain now says that the bantering between them was merely "political rhetoric." John McCain is well aware that he will need the vote of Falwell's "conservative right" if he enters the 2008 presidential race. He was invited as the guest speaker at the Liberty University May 2006 graduation. The following newspaper article [in part] discusses this rekindled relationship between the two.

"McCain to Speak at Liberty"

U.S. Senator John McCain—a likely 2008 presidential candidate who once labeled the Rev. Jerry Falwell an "agent of intolerance"—will be Liberty University's graduation speaker on May 13. "I was in Washington with him about three months ago," Falwell said. "We dealt with every difference we have. There are no deal breakers now. But I told him, 'You have a lot of fence mending to do.'"

Falwell, Liberty University's chancellor, said McCain, an Arizona Republican is among the presidential candidates he could support in 2008. "This is not an endorsement," Falwell said. McCain, 69, was out of his Washington office on Monday and could not be reached for comment.

McCain's visit to the Liberty University campus is, at the very least, an attempt to make peace with conservative Christians prior to the presidential campaign. While running against then-Governor George W. Bush in the South Carolina and Virginia primaries in 2000, McCain denounced Falwell and Virginia Beach televangelist Pat Robertson in what was seen as a move to lure more moderate voters to his campaign. "Neither party should be defined by pandering to the outer reaches of American politics and the agents of intolerance, whether they be Louis Farrakhan or Al Sharpton on the left or Pat Robertson or Jerry Falwell on the right," McCain said at the time. McCain lost the Virginia and South Carolina primaries and Bush won the nomination. This year, some polls show McCain as the early front-runner for the Republican nomination in the campaign to become Bush's successor.

Falwell said McCain's appearance at Liberty University's graduation indicates that McCain is wooing evangelical Christians. "He is in the process of healing the breach with evangelical groups," Falwell said. He also said McCain has expressed a willingness to support a Federal Marriage Amendment, an issue dear to conservative Christians.

The amendment would define marriage as a union between one man and one woman. Christian conservatives, including Falwell, are concerned about efforts by homosexual groups to have civil unions between same-sex partners recognized as marriages. McCain previously has said the matter of defining marriage should be handled by state legislatures, but now concedes that a federal statute may be necessary, Falwell said.

Aside from their political skirmishes, Falwell said McCain is an authentic American hero. "On this, everybody agrees," he said. "We weren't opposed to John McCain in 2000," Falwell said. "We were more supporters of George Bush. But I'm not going to be endorsing anyone until after November's election."[87]

"Inner Circle"

In order to be a strong leader one needs to be surrounded by reputable and credible people. Jerry Falwell does not have an entourage with these credentials.

- A Liberty University professor and personal confidant to Falwell has on several occasions, allegedly, slept with his sister-in-law.
- A close friend and former lawyer for Jerry Falwell Ministries was convicted of fraud and faces prison.
- A Methodist minister, friend, and former mayor of Lynchburg has been convicted of mail and social security fraud.
- Liberty University and Thomas Road Baptist Church are growing in numbers, but are spiritually stagnant.

"Charles Gilman Lowry"

In January 2006, the Virginia State Bar permanently revoked the law license of a Lynchburg attorney, Charles Gilman Lowry, amidst a guilty plea to federal fraud charges. He was convicted of a scheme involving wire fraud and conspiracy to commit wire fraud and defraud the IRS. Prosecutors said Lowry exploited people's Christian faith and trust in his office to get them to invest millions in the conspiracy.

Charles Lowry was the lawyer for Thomas Road Baptist Church and Liberty University for a number of years, as well as a personal friend of Dr. Falwell's, both past and present. He was also in charge of the Estate Planning Department according to my dear friend, Thomas Arnold, who now heads the department. The Estate Planning Department sells charitable gift annuities and other investments to make and raise money for Liberty University and Thomas Road Baptist Church. To me this sounds more like a business than a church.

A recent article excerpted below gives the details and fate of Lowry and his "partner in crime."

"Pair Off to Prison for Investment Fraud Roles"

Two local men were sentenced Friday for running a fraudulent investment scheme that bilked at least nine people out of more than $2 million. Charles Gilman Lowry, 74, of Lynchburg, was sentenced in U.S. District Court to two years and nine months in prison on one count each of wire fraud and conspiracy to commit wire fraud.

Charles Monroe Grooms, 46, of Madison Heights, was sentenced to two years and six months in prison on the same charges plus one count of health care fraud for lying about his income when applying for Medicaid and food stamps.

U.S. District Judge Norman Moon called Lowry, whom prosecutors described as the scheme's mastermind, a "consummate con man, an evil con man."

"To steal people's life savings is just absolutely the worst thing anybody can do," Moon said.

Lowry and Grooms were charged in February 2005 with convincing at least nine people between 1999 and 2004 to give them roughly $3 million for what they said were risk-free opportunities, promising returns of up to 8 percent through their company High Yield Inc. The pair claimed the investments were safe because the money would stay in trust accounts and only be used as collateral for high-yield bonds, said Heidi Coy, spokeswoman for the U.S. Attorney's Office. However, they never delivered the promised returns, according to prosecutors' evidence detailed in court documents. Lowry used some of the money to buy a Dodge Durango sport utility vehicle for his daughter and a Honda Accord for his wife.

Lowry and Grooms moved the money among multiple U.S. and offshore bank accounts without telling investors and faked tax returns, among other things, prosecutors said. When some investors asked Lowry to give their money back, he repeatedly refused, assured them the money was safe and said they would see the promised returns soon, prosecutors said. Assistant U.S. Attorney Patrick Hogeboom III said Lowry, an attorney at the time, was chiefly responsible for convincing others to go along with the plan. "He had the law license, he had the connections, he was bringing people in," Hogeboom said.

Lowry and Grooms played on the investors' Christian faith to gain credibility and told them not to tell others of the plans, prosecutors said. Lowry assured one family he could be trusted with $1 million because he was a Christian. A member of that family, Robert Michaels, said in court Friday falling victim to the scheme was "a never-ending nightmare.... I've listened to years of excuses and promises," Michaels said.

Lowry and Grooms convinced an Amish family to put up its farm for investment money, prosecutors said. In 2003, a woman gave the pair $1 million after they told her the money would help pay for schools and orphanages in Afghanistan and Peru, prosecutors said. She recovered about $500,000 after months of threatening legal action. Lowry defended the investment plans Friday as legitimate opportunities that didn't pan out. Lowry's attorney, Paul Beers, said Lowry himself was defrauded by others involved.

"I made a mistake that I shouldn't have made," Lowry said, "but I had personal guarantees that I wouldn't lose a dime."

"It's no mistake," Moon countered. "It's a deliberate fraud."

Lowry and Grooms had faced more than a dozen charges and decades in prison. In exchange for the pair's guilty pleas in January, prosecutors dropped most of the charges and agreed to seek a relatively light sentence. The two must pay back more than the $2 million still owed to their investors.[88]

> *"It is not the one who has too little, but the one who craves more, that is poor."*
>
> —Seneca

"The Falwell Offices"

Is corruption present within the Falwell Empire? I do not know for certain. However, I do know that the $32,500 given Mayor Carl Hutcherson was wrong, immoral, and ungodly for at least two reasons. First of all, I believe the money donated to Hutcherson was to buy votes and influence as mayor on the city council. The Falwells have on various occasions requested that land be rezoned for their building projects and retail developments. Such requests continually occur. This is possibly one way to get the land rezoned in their favor. Secondly, the money donated to Hutcherson by Jerry Falwell Ministries was probably given by supporters of the ministry to be used for that purpose.

In any event, the FBI saw fit to wiretap telephone lines at the Falwell offices on the campus of Liberty University. The details are accounted in the following news article.[89]

"FBI Recorded Hutcherson Conversation"

An FBI agent taped a telephone conversation between Jerry Falwell Jr. and Lynchburg Mayor, Carl Hutcherson in January 2005 without Falwell Jr.'s knowledge, a government motion filed Tuesday revealed. Falwell Jr. said Tuesday evening that the government only recently told him that the call was recorded. "It was a surprise to me," Falwell Jr. said. "But everything in that conversation is consistent with what we said later."

The mayor faces fraud charges related to a $32,500 donation from the Falwell ministries alleging that he used the money to improperly pay off tax debts, then lied to cover up his actions.

The fourteen page document, filed Tuesday, says the government investigated "the possibility of public corruption by covertly recording a telephone call placed by Hutcherson at the government's direction to Jerry Falwell Jr."

The thirteen minute conversation taped on January 27, 2005—the same day Hutcherson was first interviewed by the FBI—focused almost exclusively on the $32,500 gift from the Falwell ministries to a church group Hutcherson directed.

"The resultant taped conversation confirmed Hutcherson's denials of a bribery scheme," the motion says. The motion continued by saying, "The taped conversation made clear that Falwell Jr. meant for the $32,500 to be a donation to Trinity CDC and not for Trinity CDC to be a mere shell or funnel for money to be given to Hutcherson."

Assistant U.S. Attorney Tom Bondurant is asking a judge to allow the conversation to be used as evidence at Hutcherson's trial, set to begin next month. Defense attorney John Fiswick said in a prepared statement that Tuesday was the first time he had a chance to see the transcript. "We have always anticipated that the contents of the conversation are supportive of our case," he said in the statement. "We can't wait for the jury to hear it." Bondurant argues that Hutcherson knew the money wasn't a loan to his funeral home.

The government says Hutcherson's defense team will likely argue that the Falwells intended the money to go to the mayor all along, so no criminal intent existed.

Prosecutors say in the motion that the "conversation is relevant because it demonstrates Hutcherson's true criminal intent and refutes his potential defense." Hutcherson made the initial contact with Falwell Jr.'s Liberty University office at 2:36 p.m. while FBI Special Agent Christian Pettyjohn was present.

The mayor begins the conversation by informing Falwell that an FBI agent was asking questions about the donation. The mayor then tells Falwell the agent "knew it was a direct loan, and uh, um, to me."

Here is one exchange between Hutcherson and Falwell Jr. from the transcript, which was posted on the web site of the federal court Tuesday along with a motion to introduce it as evidence.

> Hutcherson: I didn't answer, I didn't answer a lot after that because uh, ultimately what they did was issue me a subpoena.
> Falwell: Is that right?
> Hutcherson: Alright, well we, it was a donation to that New Life, that's who we made the check out to, right?
> Hutcherson: Yes, uh huh.
> Falwell: So what's, I don't understand what's wrong with that."
> Hutcherson: I don't, I don't know.

Over the course of the conversation, Falwell repeatedly says the money was given as a donation to the CDC, not a personal loan.

"They're just uh, but I just uh, I can't think, Carl, what it would be that uh, would be so bad," Falwell said. "Even if we had just loaned the funeral home."

Falwell also refers to the Ericsson rezoning on the north campus of Liberty University from the year before that initially drew the attention of federal investigators.

From the transcript:

Falwell: But at the time you voted on that rezoning for us, it was nothing, no business relationship at all.
Hutcherson: That's, no, no. There wasn't. No.
Falwell: They're just trying to scare you.

Falwell said Tuesday that the Bank of the James, the institution where the donation was deposited, was responsible for the entire investigation beginning.

From the transcript:

Falwell: Now, it's probably Bank of the James that's brought that up. Hutcherson: Probably so.
Falwell: Oh, yeah. I don't trust those people.

A related newspaper article highlights several criminal charges that could be lodged against the mayor.

- Social Security Fraud
- Mail Fraud
- Bank Fraud
- Making a False Statement to a Federal Official
- Obstruction of Justice

A jury deliberated less than two hours before finding Mayor Hutcherson guilty on all counts of fraud, perjury, and obstruction charges. In addition to serving as mayor, Hutcherson served as pastor of Trinity United Methodist Church and ran a funeral home. He set up a charity, Trinity New Life Community Development Corporation, and moved donated gifts into his business bank account. This included a $32,500 gift from the Falwell Ministries.[90]

> *"I hope I shall possess firmness and virtue enough to maintain what I consider the most enviable of all titles, the character of an honest man."*
> —George Washington

"Racism"

Is Liberty University a racist institution? Falwell was reared to believe that segregation was the natural order of things. However, he changed his view as a young pastor and began baptizing blacks in the early 1960s. Still, the faculty of his Lynchburg Christian Academy is all white, and among 1,147 pupils enrolled this semester, only five are black. Where his schools are concerned, he admits: "I don't think we've gone after blacks aggressively."[91]

I don't know for sure that Falwell changed his view about blacks in the early 1960s. However, I do know for sure that the policy of the school and college in the early 1970s was that blacks and whites COULD NOT DATE. This policy was later changed because of outside pressures. However, the mentality is still very much present.

"Bigotry"

Is the Falwell philosophy threaded with bigotry? You decide from the following articles.

"Falwell Says He Once Didn't Have a Problem with Abortion, Gays"

The Rev. Jerry Falwell told members of the First Baptist Church that, while growing up in a home with an agnostic father, he didn't show animosity toward homosexuals or abortion. "I never had a problem with abortion or gay marriage until I became a Christian because I never confronted anyone about it before then," Falwell said. "But the things that were true fifty years ago are still true today. Violating God's principles brings a nation or family to shame, but following them will make you great in the way the Lord wants you to be great." Falwell is the founder of the Thomas Road Baptist Church and Liberty University in Lynchburg, Virginia." I was not raised in the home of a Baptist preacher. I didn't even own a Bible when I got saved," Falwell said. "My father was agnostic and one of the largest distributors of whiskey during Prohibition. He was also the sheriff, but he died from overindulgence of alcohol by the time he was in his mid-50s." In his address, Falwell lamented the nation's high divorce rate and absentee fathers. "A fifty percent divorce rate is unacceptable. Somehow we must get attention of the fathers as to their priestly responsibility to their wives and children and that has to be done through the local churches," he said.[92]

"Gay Rights Group Aims for LU—Falwell Says
Soulforce Not Allowed at School" (in part)

On Friday, a group of gay rights activists may risk jail to come to Liberty University. The Soulforce Equality Ride, a seven-week bus tour visiting nineteen religious colleges and military academies that ban the enrollment of lesbian, gay, bisexual and transgender students, will make its first stop at LU. Thirty-five people will participate in the ride, and co-director Jake Reitan said that as many as one hundred people could join them in Lynchburg. But their presence will not be welcome. LU has issued a statement from the Rev. Jerry Falwell saying that the Equality Ride, which visited the campus last April in a trial run, will not be allowed to return to LU as a "media demonstration."

"The parents of our students have entrusted their sons and daughters to our care," Falwell said in the statement. "Liberty has an obligation to these parents not to expose their children to a 'media circus' that might present immorality in a positive light." A release from Soulforce, the organization behind the ride, quotes LU Police Chief Randy Smith as saying, "Soulforce will not be allowed on the property and this will be enforced by arrest if needed. Smith was not available for comment, and LU did not comment beyond Falwell's initial release. Reitan said that Falwell's decision could backfire. "The reality is, they're creating the media circus by trying to arrest us," Reitan said. "When they deny our visit and try to arrest us, they show their true colors." Reitan said the Equality Ride will also visit such campuses as Brigham Young University and Oral Roberts University, and include presentations and open discussion with students about homosexuality. He said that he was inspired to start the ride by a gay student he met while attending Northwestern University. Reitan said that the student, who attended Wheaton College, discussed the school's anti-homosexual policy and his fear of expulsion for being gay. I said, "That's a terrible policy, we should do something about it," and he said, 'I think it's a great policy. It's a sin to be gay,' " Reitan recalled. He said that one of the goals of the ride was to help reach gay students on religious campuses. He said they were being told that who they were made them an affront to God. Soulforce is a locally based organization committed to "ending the stigmatization of gay, lesbian, bisexual, and transgender people—stigmatization caused by religion-based bias." The organization was cofounded by the Rev. Mel White, a former ghostwriter for Falwell who came out as a homosexual in 1993. Falwell said in the statement that he had permitted Soulforce to meet with LU representatives last year, and allowed a delegation of 150 people from Soulforce to engage in dialogue at the campus church on another occasion. He said that he felt that Soulforce was not acting in good faith with this visit, and would "use such encounters on Christian college campuses as a media attraction and for their ultimate purpose of fundraising." Reitan said that Soulforce just wanted to enter into a dialogue with people at LU. "I don't know if they're going to change their hearts and minds," Reitan said. "I hope at least they'll change their preconceptions of what it is to be gay and lesbian." The Equality

Ride will meet at First Christian Church on Friday at 9:30 a.m. A service will be held at 7 p.m. on Thursday.[93]

On the day of the march twenty-four activists were arrested.

"Double Standard"

Over the years, Lynchburg, Virginia, home of Liberty University, has lost numerous industries and jobs along with them. Being a conservative area with above average unemployment, Lynchburg offers many low-wage jobs. A large portion of the population works two or more jobs to support their families, especially with gas prices and other essentials rising constantly when wages are not. The parochial, supposedly Christian university hops on the bandwagon and pays sub-average wages. In fact, many workers are paid the minimum wage. The management constantly emphasizes that you are working for a ministry, and therefore, they cannot pay the workers much. The ministry keeps most of the employees poor except the ones at the top—they are made rich. This is because the top of the so-called ministry operates like any other business.

There is a constant emphasis on growth and increased student enrollment. Why? Because growth means more money and prestige for the top people. This is not Christian or biblical, as demonstrated in the scriptures set out below.

> *"The laborer is worthy of his hire . . ."*
> —Luke 10:7

> *"Any that provides not for his own . . . is worse than an infidel."*
> —I Timothy 5:8

> *"Lord, grant that I may seek rather to comfort, than to be comforted—to understand, than to be understood—to love, than to be loved—for it is by giving that one receives."*
> —St Francis of Assisi.

"Falwell Influence"

Dr. Jerry Falwell is a very influential man. He is responsible for filling to capacity the gas stations, shopping malls, restaurants, and hotels in the Lynchburg area. Thus, he has his way with the local business owners, the local city council, and in some instances, the local courts. I always believed pastors should be shepherds of the flock, and not power controllers over the masses.

A number of years ago Falwell was the major force behind the city council not allowing a civic center to locate in Lynchburg. This allows Falwell to control the entertainment and the money coming to the city, since Liberty University is home to the Vines Center, which seats nearly ten thousand people. The Vines Center is the largest arena within a fifty-mile radius of Lynchburg.

On July 4, 2006, Jerry Falwell's Thomas Road Baptist Church moved to its new facility on the campus of Liberty University. This new edifice is now considered a 'super church' and functions similarly to major corporations. The evolution of Thomas Road from a place of worship to a social service center has come under government authority in matters affecting zoning, parking, educational practices, and day care facilities. What used to be called chapel service is now called convocation, and gospel music is now contemporary Christian Rock. Being bigger is rarely better.

"Manipulation"

New facilities, more staff positions, a greater communication network, and higher wages for the elite requires more and more sophisticated marketing techniques to raise money. This high-pressure marketing along with human psychology equals manipulation. "Give until it hurts," they say. God will ultimately bless you. If you do not give your ten percent and MORE, then you are a thief. This sort of fundraising is wrong, immoral, and ungodly. It employs sinful pressure tactics that are placed on parishioners by ungodly preachers and charismatic leaders.

The following are the true six principles of giving:

1) Compassionately
2) Responsively
3) Cheerfully
4) Proportionally
5) Sacrificially
6) Spontaneously.

It has been proven that the rich give the least in proportion. Have you seen any televangelists at the local "soup kitchens?" All are very, very wealthy.

> *"Character is like a tree and reputation is like its shadow. The shadow is what we think of it; the tree is the real thing."*
> —Abraham Lincoln

CHAPTER 12

LAST DAYS

"You'll never recognize the devil if you expect him to have horns."
—English Proverb

"And you shall hear of wars and rumors of wars: see that you be not troubled: for all these things must come to pass, but the end is not yet. For nation shall rise against nation and kingdom against kingdom: and there shall be famines, and pestilences and earthquakes, in divers places. All these are the beginning of sorrows," (Matthew 24: 6-8). We could also add to this list the following: global warming, tsunamis, pandemics, and TERRORISM. Presently there is much in the way of destruction, and much being written about these events; however, biblical scholars and writers have missed the picture entirely on why all of these tragedies are going on. Manifold prognosticators of sorts can biblically claim to give you the future plan for world events but all are equivocally blinded as to why disastrous events are presently unfolding.

From page one of this book, my thesis has been the unethical fundraising, the love of money, and the political involvements of our "so-called" conservative religious right. How the primary goal of these godless emissaries has never been to tend the flock, but merely to fleece the sheep. They are selling religion in order to harness personal wealth and to ensure their own legacy. Personally, I feel my thesis has been strongly vindicated and that the verdict is in. Guilty! Guilty! Guilty!

Now, what exactly does all this mean for America? And what role will America, if any, play in the end times? And who or what will be responsible for America's demise?

Mammon

Webster defines mammon as riches regarded as an object of worship and greedy pursuit, wealth or material gain as an evil, more or less deified. Christ spoke and personified mammon as riches sought to be a life goal oppose to God, (Matt. 6:24 and Luke 16:13). Thus, when people become opposed to God, they then associate themselves to the devil.

"For the love of money is the root of all evil: which while some coveted after, they have erred from the faith, and pierced themselves through many sorrows," (1 Tim. 6:10). First Timothy along with second Timothy and Titus have been designated the Pastoral Epistles. They were written by Paul the Apostle as guidelines and instructions primarily to pastors. Are pastors seeking wealth today? Sure they are! Have they erred from the truth? Sure they have! Will this affect America in the last days? It most certainly will!

If you dig deep into societal evil you will find the love of money. America's churches have become "big business." The context of First Timothy 6:10 adds much evidence to this conclusion. The desire of our ecclesiastical leadership for money leads them into other evils; evils like cheating, bribing, lying, and immoral living. They are greatly more susceptible to many lustful temptations because of their love and desire for more and more money. Preachers today say that "gain is godliness." This false preaching is prevalent to keep the grounds and their salaries. This is sinful and its root lies in the love of money.

Oppressions of the Rich

The Book of James is written to believers and the context is about pure religion.

> Go to now, you rich men, weep and howl for your miseries that shall come upon you. Your riches are corrupted, and your garments are moth eaten. Your gold and silver is cankered; and the rust of them shall be a witness against you, and shall eat your flesh as it were fire. You have heaped treasure together for the LAST DAYS.
>
> Behold, the hire of the labourers who have reaped down your fields, which is of you kept back by fraud, crieth: and the cries of them which have reaped are entered into the ears of the Lord of Sabaoth. You have lived in pleasure on the earth, and been wanton; you have nourished your hearts, as in a day of slaughter. You have condemned and killed the just; and he doth not resist you. James 5:1-6

Satan is also called the Devil, the Adversary, the Enemy, the Accuser, the Evil One, and the God of this World. Satan is the personification of evil in the heart. He is worldly minded and distorts the truth. Are our religious personalities distorting the truth today? Why yes they are! Knowingly or unknowingly they are the false prophets of Satan's Trinity. Their prime concern is money or mammon; and Satan is also synonymous with mammon throughout the Bible. Thus the Apocalypse—last days or end times—especially depicts the passion of Satan and his prophets, particularly in the future as he affects the church. His false prophets are unrelenting at deception and masters of seducing people to evil and ruin while engaged in a worldwide struggle against God. Their message is not goodness but GOLD. Their power over people is held by virtue of usurpation.

Puppets of Satan

"Satan has assumed the position of god—substitute for this world. The world in Scripture really means materialism: the system of living that is organized without God and that acts on the assumption that all reality is bounded by the horizons of birth and death. We therefore live so as to get the maximum out of this life and lay up treasure on earth. Thus the 'world' is not the same as the 'earth,' which in all its fullness is the Lord's (Ps 24:1).

We must, however, listen to the warnings of Christ and the New Testament writers that Satan has another line of attack, namely, persuading the church to shift from the basic revealed beliefs. Jesus Christ warned of false messiahs and false prophets who would be a menace to the faith of the church."[94]

For there shall arise false Christ, and false prophets, and shall show great signs and wonders; insomuch that, if it were possible, they shall deceive the very elect. Matt. 24:24

These false prophets and preachers of heresy will throw a veil of darkness over the minds and hearts of men. Their manipulation and gains—seeking ventures is no more than the occult of greediness.

Apostasy

Apostasy can be defined as the "falling away" or "departure from the truth of one's belief and principles." These hypocritical false preachers and pretenders are filling many pulpits around America today. They use the right language and promote love, yet they are merely gains-seekers. They lead astray those who willingly and ignorantly follow them.

"The whole second chapter of Second Peter is given over to a description of false teachers, and one thing that stands out is the immoral quality of their lives. 'And many will follow their sensuality' (v.2); 'those who indulge the flesh in its corrupt desires (v.10); and 'speaking out arrogant words of vanity, they entice by fleshly desires, by sensuality' (v.18). Peter mentions these apostates again later (3:3) and says, 'know this first of all, that in the last days mockers will come with their mocking, following after their own lusts.' Jim Jones is a graphic reminder of this."[95]

These false teachers are motivated by power and money. They have become wealthy off other people; they are in the ministry for the money. These ministers of evil are fleecing the sheep instead of tending to the flock. The motivation is lust and self-satisfaction. They promise plenty and deliver nothing.

> "That you may be mindful of the words which ere spoken before by the holy prophets, and of the commandments of us the apostles of the Lord and Saviour: knowing this first, that there shall come in the LAST DAYS scoffers, walking after their own lusts." II Peter 3:2, 3

The Lukewarm Church

Most of our modern-day church is falling away from Biblical Christianity and are hastily substituting ungodly doctrines and demonic philosophies in its place. The holy writings have thoroughly warned that this would happen in the LAST DAYS.

> He that hath an ear, let him hear what the Spirit saith unto the churches. And unto the angel of the church of the Laodiceans write; these things saith the Amen, the faithful and true witness, the beginning of the creation of God; I know thy works, that thou art neither cold, nor hot: I would thou to be cold or hot. So then because thou art lukewarm, and neither cold nor hot, I will spue thee out of my mouth. Because thou sayest, I am rich, and increased with goods, and have need of nothing, and knowest not that thou art wretched, and miserable, and poor, and blind, and naked:...I rebuke and chasten: be zealous therefore, and repent. Revelation 3:13-17, 19

"The Laodicean condition describes the spiritual lukewarmness and worldliness which will prevail in the professing church of Christ at the end of the age. Rich, cultured, religious ritualistic—this church will have become so self-satisfied and worldly, as to have ostracized prophetically as standing on the outside knocking for admission (Rev. 3:20). No longer is he admitted by the corporate body, but stands outside extending an invitation to individuals."[96]

My question is: Have the churches and her leadership failed? The church is an American institution with a very real moral responsibility; however, they too have failed to provide moral rulership and because their accountability is the greatest, their failure is the most harmful.

The church that thus defines her strength is on the speedway to apostasy. The modern day doomed church has transferred her strength from spiritual to material, from holy living to worldly living. Her humility, meekness, and reverence have been replaced with pride, power, and reproach.

The modern church has its parlor and kitchen, its clubs, its clicks and lyceum; ministering to the flesh and to the world, is both suggestive and appalling. How insinuating in the contrast it presents between the agencies which the early church originated and nourished, as the conserver of its principles, and the expression of its life, and those which the contemporary and progressive church presents as its allies or surrogates. The original institutions were totally spiritual, computed to cultivate and strengthen all the components which combine to make an acute and obvious experience of God. They were instructing schools for the spiritual life, submissive to its culture as the principle end. These churches never loitered in the regions of the mental, the moral, or the sensitive. They adopted no taste nor inclination which was not spiritual, and did not minister to the soul's progress in divine affairs.

Also, we can add to the register of heavenly helpers, a gymnasium, a skating rink, and a multipurpose center for rock concerts. If the young people desire to join a club, a lyceum, or enjoy a sociable, let them do so, however, tend not to deceive them and downgrade piety by calling these affairs holy institutions and food for spiritual life. Numerous preachers and charismatic leaders in the church have fallen so low in their experience that they do not delight in any distinct and impregnable agencies. They are devising schemes and organizations to gratify their non-spiritual relishments with programs with are halfway between Christ and the world; which, while not intrinsically wrong, do not possess one grain of spiritual power, and can never be the arteries of heavenly communications.

Satan is alive and doing very well in our modern-day ecclesiastical giants. Our televangelists and religious right—preaching politics and prosperity—have all but united with the Devil as his messengers of false prophecy. The Church cannot confederate with non-spiritual agencies. By doing this, she splinters the tension of her faith and scraps the Holy Spirit. She cannot be the purveyor to unholy desires. This is her most doleful mistake, when her solemn assemblies are abandoned to the concert and lecture, her glory and praise turned into worldly music, her classrooms into parlors, her social-meetings become more popular than her prayer meetings, the house of God made into a house of feasting, and social gaiety is sought after rather than a house of prayer. The oneness of the spirit and the holy brotherhood are transported and destroyed to make room for hospitable affinities and worldly attractions.

> And Jesus went into the temple of god, and cast out all them that sold and bought in the temple and overthrew the tables of the moneychangers, and the seats of them that sold doves. And said unto them, it is written, My house shall be called the house of prayer; but you have made it a den of thieves. Matthew 21:12, 13

Signs of the Times

In the last days, according to the Bible the antichrist will govern everything we hear, see and do. The stage is now being established. Events are taking shape and the worst is yet to come. Read and comprehend the following in order to better anticipate and cope with future occurrences and their catastrophes.

- Wars and rumors of wars   Yes
- Earthquakes in many places   Yes

- Famines and food shortages   Yes
- Natural disasters   Yes
- Widespread deception   Yes
- Apostasy and false preaching   Yes
- Armageddon   Not Yet

These are real happenings set forth in prophecy having to do with the consummation of the times in which we are living. Read and heed and compare them with the events of which our local and national papers are crammed with. May you recall the challenging question stated by our Lord to the religious leaders of this day: "Can you not discern the signs of the times? (Matt. 16:3).

1) "And you shall hear of wars and rumors of wars: see that you be not troubled: for all these things must come to pass, but the end is not yet" (Matt. 24:6).

Christ is speaking here from the Mount of Olives. He is saying that the "time is not yet." If you listen to the religious prognosticators of today, one might expect that they can predict the end of the world. This is far from the truth. Jesus said: "No man knows the day nor the hour." We have had wars for thousands of years; however, they are becoming much more prevalent today.

Human history saw our first global war in 1914. This was followed in 1939 by our second global war. Since World War II the increase of wars and rumors of wars is certainly of universal concern. In fact there are approximately two to three dozen wars—in various degrees and sizes—around the world annually. However, the Second Coming of Christ will not be in worldwide war, but will be when the world's economy is in ruins and peace on the horizon.

2) Greatly increased natural disasters: "For nation shall rise against kingdom: and there shall be famines, and pestilences and earthquakes, in divers places" (Matt. 24:7).

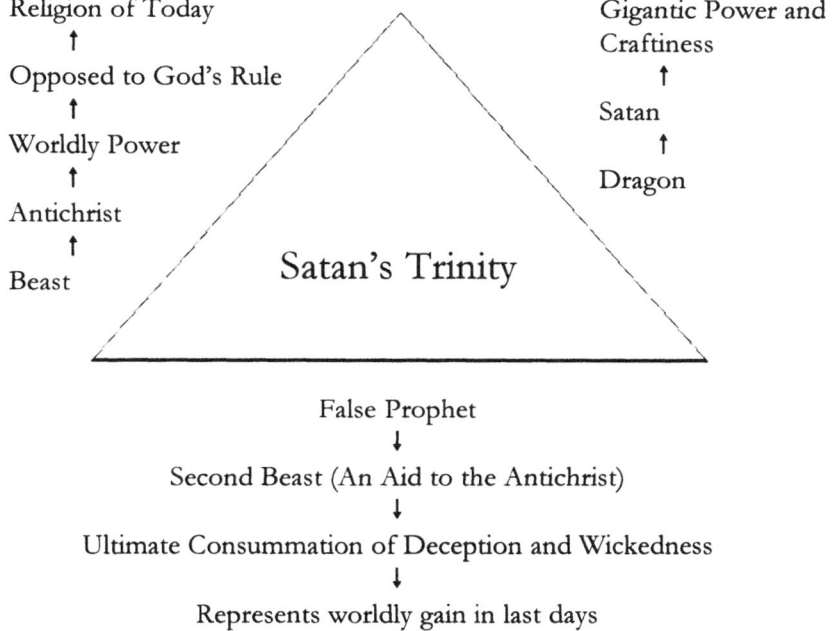

Devastating hurricanes, tsunamis, earthquakes, and global warming are definitely on the increase. However, this is not the end. Remember that Jesus said "all these are the beginning of sorrows." Circumstances can and probably will worsen before they worldwide economic decay unfolds.

3) Famines and food shortages will greatly increase. Our present world has not seen nor is it prepared for the great devastating plagues which are to come. The desolation that was unleashed upon Egypt and Pharaoh in the Old Testament will ultimately be unshackled on the present-day world. Ultimate destruction will be worldwide.

4) Apostasy, false preaching and widespread deception will be the greatest sign in the LAST DAYS. Not only the greatest sign, but also the most dangerous for America.

"Knowing this first, that there shall come in the last days scoffers, walking after their own lusts" (II Peter 3:3).

"Beware of false prophets, which come to you in sheep's clothing, but inwardly they are ravening wolves" (Matt. 7:15).

"And many false prophets shall rise, and shall deceive many" (Matt. 24:11).

Who are these false prophets? Are they people of little renown with a small voice with the masses? No! No! No! They are powerful, well—known religious leaders of our television world. They are preaching the false message of "health and wealth" and placing all their energies and pursuit into establishing a personal legacy. They are fleecing the sheep and Christ had much to say about this.

"Lay not up for yourselves treasures upon earth...No man can serve two masters: for either he will hate the one, and love the other; or else he will hold to the one, and despise the other. You cannot serve God and mammon" (Matt 6:19, 24).

Who are they and where do these self-seekers fit into prophecy?
"In close association with the Beast, the head of the federated empire, is anther individual known as the 'False Prophet' (Rev. 19:20; 20:10), called 'the second beast' in Revelation 13:11-17. It will be observed that the Revelation, in relating the second beast to the first, presents him as subservient to the first. He is called 'the false prophet' (Rev. 16:13; 19:20; 20:10), who ministers is connection with the first beast as his prophet or spokesman. We are presented, then, with a satanic trinity, of hell: the dragon, the Beast, and the False Prophet (Rev. 16:13). That place

occupied by God in His program is assumed by Satan, that place of Christ is assumed by the first Beast, that ministry of the Holy Spirit is discharged by the False Prophet."[97]

The Two Beasts

The most renown of New Testament and the one that uses "False Prophet" as a proper noun is the Book of Revelation. In this end time's prophecy, the False Prophet prepares the way for the Beast. This False Prophet is not a literal person or one single voice, but a great world religious federation displaying great power: "for many shall come in my name, saying I am Christ; and shall deceive many. For there shall arise false Christs, and false prophets, and shall show great signs and wonders; insomuch that, if it were possible, they shall deceive the very elect" (Matt. 24:5, 24). Remember the chapter "Orbis Unum"? This is the religious federation—the false prophet or second beast—that is aligning itself with sundry coalitions around the world today. These, coalitions are "money driven" and portray religion as largely a matter of form and wealth: "This know also, that in the last days perilous times shall come. For men shall be lovers of their own selves, covetous, boasters, proud, blasphemers, unthankful, unholy, having a form of godliness, but denying the power thereof: from such turn away" (II Tim. 3:1-2, 5). Does this not sound like our infamous religious personalities of today who are "selling religion" and incorporating wealth and politics into their sermons?

The Beast and the False Prophet are confederates—one political, the other religious. They will work hand-in-hand perfectly. The Beast will head the civil power, while the False Prophet—Second Beast—will be the religious authority. A conglomerate or federation energized by Satan.

And I beheld another beast coming up out of the earth; and he had two horns like a ram, and he spoke as a dragon. Revelation 13:11

TIMELINE OF HISTORY

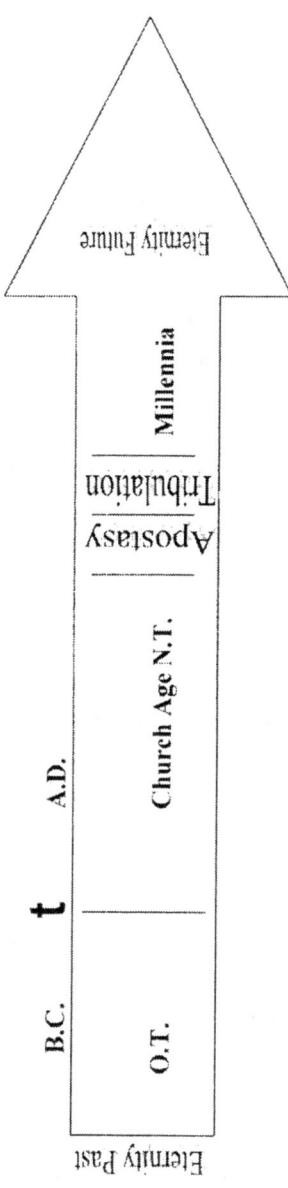

These two horns of the Second Beast represent the political and religious power being amassed by the "one great world religion" being constructed today. Be NOT deceived!

5) Global warming is a documented and observed increase—over the last several decades—in the average temperature of the Earth's oceans, and atmosphere. This was predicted 2,000 years ago by the Apostle Peter as a sign of the last days.

But the heavens and the earth, which are now, by the same word are kept in store, reserved unto fire against the Day of Judgment and perdition of ungodly men. But the day of the Lord will come as a thief in the night; in the which the heavens shall pass away with a great noise, and the elements shall melt with fervent heat, the earth also and the works that are therein shall be burned up. II Peter 3:7, 10

An increase in global temperatures will cause a domino effect in the world's climate with catastrophic results including:

1. Droughts and fires
2. Flooding and heavy snow
3. Hurricanes and tornadoes
4. Lower agriculture yield
5. Famines
6. Spreading of disease
7. Glacier retreat
8. Plant and animal range shifts
9. Population changes

The increase of severe and violent climatic events, combined with social trends could cost the United States billions of dollars annually, in the next decade. Thus, the financial costs of global warming associated with insurance and disaster relief would burden all aspects of our economy. Tax payers and industry alike would foot the bill.

Our coastlines exhibit large numbers of people, as well as, expensive real estate. They are very vulnerable to tsunamis, hurricanes, and rising ocean's water levels, all connected to global warming. Are we prepared? Can we change the course of events?

What About America?

"You are the salt of the earth: but if the salt have lost his savor, wherewith shall it be salted? It is thenceforth good for nothing, but to be cast out, and to be trodden under foot of men" Matthew 5:13

"Live free, or die."
—New Hampshire State Motto

America was born in freedom and liberty to live in peace and worship as we please. The puritans ventured to this new land to escape religious control by the Church of England. America over the last several centuries has been great, however, many of our religious leaders are destined to make "the land of the free" into their own national theocracy through attaining power politically and monetarily. How will this affect America in the End Time? Most of the Evangelical church is steadily falling away from Biblical Christianity and are diligently substituting all types of ungodly doctrines and even demonic philosophies in its place. Dispensationalist writer Hal Lindsey calls this generation "the terminal generation."

GOP political strategist Karl Rove helped mobilize nearly twenty million fundamentalist voters in 2004 to sweep George Bush back into office. What have the fundamentalists gotten in return? Higher gas prices and wars around the world. If the leadership of the "religious right" wants Holy Crusades; then let them fight them. No! They just want a rich legacy and let you fight the wars. So-called "Christian politics" has as its primary objective the conquest and Christianization of America. However, this will not happen in the Apocalypse—End Times—because these Christian fundamentalists only seek power and self-interests, something Christ never did.

"The United States of America has aligned itself with the nations of western Europe. Some conclude that because the United States is not specifically named in the prophetic Scriptures it will be either completely destroyed or a second-rate power when this final confederacy of nations appears on the scene. This is not necessarily a correct deduction. It is quite possible perhaps even probably that the United States will play a significant role in the empire under the domination of Antichrist."[98]

We have previously demonstrated that the False Prophet—the second Beast—is indeed an aid to and under the control of the Anti-Christ. This is because the false prophet represents worldly gain—money—in the LAST DAYS. Our infamous religious leaders are preaching a false or "prosperity gospel", certainly not the Biblical John 3:16 gospel.

The following article "America in Bible Prophecy" by Jack Kinsella is excerpted with permission.

> For years well-meaning Christians have tried to find some reference to America in Bible prophecy. The most convincing argument I've heard to date is Ezekiel's reference to the 'merchants of Tarshish and all the young lions thereof' (Ezekiel 38:13). 'Tarshish is either a Sanskrit or Aryan word meaning 'sea coast.' The identity 'merchants of Tarshish' is a subject of wide debate with some scholars putting it on the European coastline to the extreme west, with others putting Tarshish on the coast of India to the east. But to find America in Tarshish, one needs to locate it on Europe's west coast, preferably in Great Britain. The 'lion' then represents Britain, and 'all the young lions thereof' can include America, a former British colony. As you can probably tell, I am skeptical of this interpretation, although it has many champions including Tommy Ice, for whom I have the utmost respect and admiration.
>
> During the Tribulation, we find references to Russia and the modern Middle East in Ezekiel's Gog Magog vision. We find references to a massive oriental power, called the Kings of the East,

capable of fielding an army of two hundred million men. (The approximate strength of the modern Chinese army, according to the CIA World Factbook.) There are references to a pan-African Alliance resembling the organization of African States, and a huge segment of prophecy is devoted exclusively to the revival of the Roman Empire and the role it plays in advancing the antichrist's agenda. But there is NO reference to anything resembling a fifth political power, especially not one as powerful alone as are the other four powers combined. That is not to say there is no mention of America in the Bible for the last days—just not during the Tribulation. I believe America represents the church in the last days, just as the nation of Israel represents Judaism.[99]

Personally, I believe America is represented by the church. However, it has become powerful and political. The Church has lost the vision and her "first love." What is the ultimate answer?

"If my people, which are called by my name, shall humble themselves, and pray, and seek my face and turn from their wicked ways; then will I hear from heaven, and will forgive their sin, and will heal their land." II Chronicles 7:14

We must as a people and as a nation become less self-centered and seek to further humanity as a whole; and not desiring a personal legacy.

I now close this chapter and this book by a great admonition from our third president.

"To do to our fellow men the most good in our power, we must lead where we can, follow where we cannot, and still go on with them, watching always for the favorable moments of helping them in another step."
—Thomas Jefferson

Endnotes:

1 "Televangelist takeover." The Nation, p. 419, April 4, 1987.

2 Barry, William. "Religious concerns with political and social questions." America. August 5, 1989, p. 61.

3 Wallis, Jim. "Who speaks for God?" USA Today. March 28, 1995.

4 Boston, Robert. The *Most Dangerous Man in America? Pat Robertson and the Rise of the Christian Coalition.* Prometheus Publishers, NY.

5 [Author name not available]. "Power, glory, and politics." Time, p. 65, February 17, 1986.

6 Saber, Erin. "Tactics of the religious right." The Christian Century, p. 782, August 11-18, 1993.

7 Wallis, Jim. Sojourners Magazine. October 1986.

8 [Author name not available]. "Is Pat Robertson raising money for anti-Sandinista guerrillas?" Christianity Today, p. 50, November 8, 1985.

9 "Pat's dictator friends." Electronic article at: http://www.geocities.com/CapitolHill/7027/patrobertson.html

10 Boston, Robert. The *Most Dangerous Man in America? Pat Robertson and the Rise of the Christian Coalition.* Prometheus Publishers, NY.

11 "Jerry Falwell's Crusade." Time Magazine, p. 49, September 2, 1985.

12 Confehr, Clint. "Jerry Falwell's Marching Christians." The Saturday Evening Post, p. 99, December 1980.

13 Lowe, Cody. "The Back Pew." Roanoke Times and World News. p.1, February 26, 1995.

14 Schleck, Dave. "Year later, Clinton video still causes fallout." The News and Advance, p. A-1, February 26, 1995.

15 Lowe, Cody. "The Back Pew." Roanoke Times and World News. p.2, February 26, 1995.

16 Baroud, R. (2006). New Lobby for Israel Created [Electronic version]. Council for the National Interest Foundation. http://www.rescuemideastpolicy.com/print.php?sid=229&.

17 Chaim, I. (2006, February 28). Falwell: Jews can get to heaven. Jerusalem Post.

18 From "The Adulation of Man in The Purpose Driven Life." (www.bereanbeacon.org). Reprinted with permission.

19 Lindsey, R. "The Difficulty in Regulating Religions that Turn a Profit."

20 Ibid.

21 Rice, J. R. False Doctrines. (1970) Murfreesboro, TN: Sword of the Lord Publishers.

22 Roberts says money prevented death. (1987, April 2). The News & Daily Advance, p. C4.

23 Facing financial charges, U.S. Orthodox orders audit. (2006, March 4). The Daily Progress, A6.

24 Gordon, M. (2001, August 7). Regulators warn on religious fraud. On-line database: http://www.sullivan-county.com

25 Schmidt, S. and Grimaldi, J.V. "Nonprofit Groups Funneled Money for Abramoff." The Washington Post, June 25, 2006, p. A1.

26 Applebome, P. "Swaggart's Troubles Show Tension of Passion and Power in TV Evangelism." The New York Times, Feb. 28, 1988.

27 "Sex Scandal and TBN." The Los Angeles Times. September 12, 2004.

28 Gumbel, A. "Scandal, sex and sanctimony." Los Angeles Times, September 18, 2004.

29 Ibid.

30 "Trinity Broadcasting Network." From Wikipedia at www.en.wikipedia.org. Accessed July 2, 2006.

31 Ibid.

32 Ibid.

33 "TBN-Trinity Broadcast Network-Temple of the Greek God and Goddess." http://www.cuttingedge.org/news/n1841.cfm. Accessed June 27, 2006.

34 Allen, Tom. "Rock 'n' Roll, the Bible and the mind." Horizon House Publishers, pp. 141-142.

35 "Sandi Patti." Christianity Today, September 11, 1995, pp. 72-74.

36 "Christian rock: Blessing or blasphemy?" Online at http://www.av1611.org/crock.html. Accessed July 2, 2006.

37 Proctor, Paul. "The Falwell Faux Pas: Another towering inferno."

38 Lindsey, Alberta. "Grab the popcorn, get set for sermon." The News & Advance, March 26, 2006. Article reprinted with permission of The News & Advance.

39 From Washington Post News Service. "From wild side to church." The Daily Progress, April 1, 2006.

40 "Jim Bakker." The Charlotte Observer, 4-19-87.

41 Michael Isikoff and Art Harvis. "Jim Bakker." The Washington Post, May 13, 1987.

42 Eleanor Clift and Mark Miller. "Reverend Moon's political moves." Newsweek, February 15, 1988, p. 31.

43 "Ex-United Way chief worked, played hard." Reprinted in its entirety with permission. The Washington Post. March 7, 1995, page A-1.

44 Susan Antilla. "Investors had faith." New York Times, June 3, 1992.

45 "Jim Bakker." The New Straits Times, October 6, 1989.

46 Knight Ridder Newspapers, September 19, 2002.

47 Online article from RaptureReady.com. http://www.rr-bb.com/showthread.php?t=197005.

48 Online article from www.seeing-stars.com.

49 Los Angeles Times, Nov 4, 2001.

50 Orange County Register, 1998. 06.

51 St. Louis Times Dispatch. STLtoday.com, November 18, 2003.

52 InPlainSite.org from The Atlanta Journal-Constitution, March 5, 2000.

53 "The Anointing." Online at http://www.inplainsite.org/html/the_anointing.html. Accessed 6-27-06.

54 The Tulsa World, April 27, 2003.

55 Online article at http://www.dallasobserver.com/issues/1997-11-06/feature2.html/page1.html

56 Analisa Nazareno. "The Exceeding Great Reward." San Antonio Express-News, June 21, 2003, 10H.

57 The Sun Herald. May. 17, 2002.

58 Online article at http://www.dentonrc.com/sharedcontent/APStories/stories/D8B5M18O0.htm

59 Coverage of Benny Hinn reported on NBC News, December 27, 2002

60 "Benny Hinn." Los Angeles Times, July 27, 2003.

61 "MinistryWatch.com recommends that donors withhold giving to Benny Hinn ministries." MinistryWatch DonorAlert, May 2005.

62 St. Louis Post-Dispatch, November 18, 2003.

63 Online article at www.trinityfi.org/press/tdjakes01.html.

64 Jim Jones. "Rising-star evangelist ministers to interracial congregation." The Fort Worth Star Telegram, August 2003.

65 Kaylois Henry. "Bishop Jakes is ready. Are you?" The Dallas Observer magazine, June 20-26, 1996, pp. 19, 22.

66 Online article from www.chicagomag.com, February 2006.

67 Carolyn Tuft and Bill Smith. St. Louis Post-Dispatch, November 16, 2003, p A1.

68 Online article from www.inplainsite.org. "Heresies in the church."

69 "Earthly empires." BusinessWeek.com.

70 Online article from www.inplainsite.org. "Heresies in the church."

71 R.L. Sumner. Book review. Give Me That Prime-Time Religion Jerry Sholes (author).

72 David Edwin Harrell, Jr. "Oral Roberts: An American life." Indiana University Press: Bloomington, IN.

73 Online article from www.inplainsite.org. "Tele-evangelist lifestyles or lifestyles of the rich and infamous." Accessed April 23, 2006.

74 Ibid.

75 Pete Evans and Todd Bates. "They're leavin' on a jet plane." www.wittenburgdoor.com.

76 Timothy Greeson. "Leadership Lifestyles of the International Churches of Christ." New Covenant Publications, March 2003.

77 A.W. Tozer. "The knowledge of the holy." Harper & Row Publishers: San Francisco, p. 66.

78 Ken Hemphill. "Mirror, mirror on the wall." Broadman Press: Nashville, TN, p. 78.

79 John Wesley Holy Club Book of Sayings: Westminster Catechisms. p. 39, Wesley Foundation: 1892. Holy Club.

80 Darr Beiser. "Mother Teresa." USA Today. January 10, 1995, p. 40.

81 Colin Greer. "Something is robbing our children of their future." Parade Magazine, March 5, 1995, p. 4.

82 Ibid.

83 Online article reprinted with permission. www.homelesspeople.com. Accessed June 23, 2006.

84 Steve Lopez. "A worthy cause, for heaven's sake." Los Angeles Times, November 7, 2001.

85 S. F. Winston. "Down and out." Christians Today, p. 21, May 2003.

86 (No author given). "Politicizing the word." Time Magazine, October 1, 1972, page 62.

87 Ron Brown. "McCain to speak at Liberty." The News & Advance, March 28, 2006, page A1.

88 Matt Busse. "Pair off to prison for investment fraud roles." The News & Advance, July 15, 2006, page A1.

89 Conor Reilly. "FBI recorded Hutcherson conversation." The News & Advance, March 29, 2006, page A1.

90 (No author given). "Mayor guilty on all counts." The News & Advance, May 3, 2006, page A1.

91 Ibid. Page 68.

92 (No author given). The News & Advance, February 14, 2006, page C10.

93 Zack Smith. The News & Advance, March 6, 2006, page A1.

94 Christianity and the Occult by J. Stafford Wright. Moody Pocket Books 1971, Chicago pp. 45, 48

95 Beware of the Pretenders by John MacArthur Jr. Victor Books, Wheaton IL 1983, p. 56

96 Unger's Bible Dictionary by Merrill F. Unger. Moody Press, Chicago p. 644, 1957

97 Things to Come by J. Dwight Pentecost. Zondervan Publishing House, Grand Rapids, Michigan, 1958, pp 336, 337.

98 Israel and the Nations in Prophecy by Richard De Haan. Zondervan Publishing House, Grand Rapids, Michigan. 1968, p. 42.

99 "America in Bible Prophecy" by Jack Kinsella. The Omega Letter, Saturday, December 17, 2005. pp 1,2.

www.ingramcontent.com/pod-product-compliance
Lightning Source LLC
Chambersburg PA
CBHW062026220426
43662CB00010B/1496